The 1862 Plot
to Kidnap Jefferson Davis

The 1862 Plot
to Kidnap Jefferson Davis

Victor Vifquain

Edited by Jeffrey H. Smith
and
Phillip Thomas Tucker

STACKPOLE
BOOKS

Published by
STACKPOLE BOOKS
5067 Ritter Road
Mechanicsburg, PA 17055

Printed in the United States of America

10 9 8 7 6 5 4 3 2 1

FIRST EDITION

Library of Congress Cataloging-in-Publication Data

Vifquain, Jean–Baptiste Victor, 1836–1904
    The 1862 plot to kidnap Jefferson Davis/Victor Vifquain;edited by Jeffery H. Smith and Phillip Thomas Tucker.
      p. cm.
    Includes bibliographical references (p.) and index.
    ISBN 0-8117-1271-0
    1. Davis, Jefferson, 1808–1889—Kidnaping, 1862. 2. Vifquain, Jean–Baptiste Victor, 1836–1904. 3. United States—History—Civil War, 1861–1865—Secret Service. 4. United States——Civil War, 1861–1865—Participation, French–American. 5. Soldiers—United States—Biography. I. Smith, Jefferey H. (Jefferey Harrison), 1943–. II. Tucker, Phillip Thomos, 1953– . III. Title.
  E467.1.D26v54 1998
  973.7'13'092—dc21   98-47427

                                            CIP

CONTENTS

PREFACE

As the twentieth century began, Victor Vifquain took a long look back at the most remarkable of his many adventures during the American Civil War. It was then, in his mid-sixties, that he wrote the book he titled *Link From A Broken Chain: Historic Reminiscences of the Civil War Relating to an Attempt to Kidnap Jeff Davis.*

The story of this fantastic enterprise, a scheme to abduct the president of the Confederacy, remained in manuscript form at the time of Vifquain's death in 1904. It passed to his wife, Caroline, and after her death in 1926 to her son Blakely Marion Vifquain. Only now, with the printing of this volume, is the book receiving its long-overdue publication. The book is an exceptional find, a rare opportunity to reveal a hitherto unknown sidelight to one of the world's most-studied wars.

The kidnap plot itself is a historical puzzle, obscured by time and little known because of its few participants and limited consequences. It was the work of a very small group of plotters—Frenchmen all—working completely in secrecy. Because the plot was not consummated, it never made headlines.

The historical record offers only tantalizing glimpses of the three principal adventurers as they traveled through Confederate Virginia in April and May of 1862. A letter written by George W. Randolph, the Confederate secretary of war, confirms that the men were held prisoner for a time in Richmond. A Confederate officer, Randolph H. McKim, relates in a postwar memoir how his soldiers encountered three Frenchmen in Virginia's Shenandoah Valley. "They were suspected of being spies," McKim wrote, "but we had no proof."

To Vifquain, writing in 1900, his undertaking of almost four decades earlier must have seemed the most romantic of episodes—like something from an Alexandre Dumas novel. And in this manner he wrote his story. Details of the kidnapping plot and the high-risk journey within the Confederacy reveal themselves in the course of the book's lively conversations, entanglements with the rebels, and idyllic interludes. For the book, Vifquain assumes the guise of the hero D'Artagnan from Dumas's *The Three Musketeers*. His companions, of course, take the names Athos, Aramis, and Porthos (though injury made Porthos miss most of the trip).

This is history told with gusto, an exuberant, ornate telling of a true tale. It is an old-fashioned story of the swashbuckling sort, full of color and drama, a supreme escapade of youth as seen through the eyes of Vifquain as he neared the end of a lifetime of accomplishment as soldier, settler, and frontier leader.

Through the drama, Vifquain keeps grounded in the events swirling about the adventurers as the Civil War enters its second year. The Union's Major General McClellan is leading his troops slowly up the Virginia Peninsula toward the Confederate capital of Richmond, and it is the progress of this advance that has everything to do with the outcome of the kidnapping scheme. As his story unfolds, Vifquain takes time to dissect the spectacular military events of the day: the Battle of Shiloh, known also as the Battle of Pittsburg Landing, and the famous clash of the ironclads *Monitor* and *Virginia* (the former *Merrimack*).

A quarter-century after Vifquain's death, his handwritten manuscript was put into typewritten form by the son named for his father's final two Civil War clashes. Blakely Marion Vifquain received his names from the battle for Fort Blakely, Alabama (for which his father was awarded the Medal of Honor), and from the attempt to ambush a Confederate train at Marion Junction, also in Alabama. On August 17, 1926, Blakely Marion Vifquain donated the typed manuscript to the Nebraska State Historical Society. As for the handwritten original, its location today is not known.

Jeffrey H. Smith first proposed to Phillip Thomas Tucker the idea of co-editing the manuscript of Smith's great-great-grandfather. Tucker was already familiar with Vifquain from his own previous books focusing on the history of the First Missouri Confederate Brigade, whose battle flag Vifquain captured at Fort Blakely.

Other connections also seemed to favor the project. Both Smith and Tucker earned their Ph.D. degrees in history at St. Louis University, also the alma mater of many members of the Missouri Brigade. And Tucker lives almost within sight of Aquia Creek in Stafford County, Virginia, where rebel cavalrymen captured Vifquain and his comrades.

The book as published here has been edited with a light hand to preserve the account as Vifquain told it. The text retains the lengthy conversations that Vifquain reconstructed novelistically as his way to enliven the story. The details of the kidnapping scheme are all here, along with digressions into the Frenchmen's amours. Only an occasional verbose or inconsequential passage is replaced by ellipsis points.

Numerous typographical and spelling errors have been corrected, occasional words were added for clarity (for example, to help distinguish between Confederate and Federal officers), and long paragraphs were broken up for ease of reading. The use of brackets and [sic] has been kept to a minimum. Reference numbers in the text refer to explanatory notes at the back of the book that flesh out the historical context of the events and their principal players.

The story is preceded by a biography of Victor Vifquain. It is quickly obvious from the biography that Vifquain's youthful foray into Richmond was characteristic of his passionate approach to life, one chapter in his pursuit of both zest and meaning during his time on earth.

ACKNOWLEDGMENTS

WE WOULD LIKE TO THANK THE MEMBERS OF THE VIFQUAIN FAMILY WHO graciously allowed the use of rare family photographs and personal papers to make this work possible. Most of all, we give our thanks to the patient and good people at Stackpole Books, including Michelle M. Simmons, associate editor, and especially premier Civil War historian William C. Davis, for their support and guidance throughout this project. From beginning to end, Mr. Davis believed in the value of this work and placed his faith in the ability of the co-editors to make it the best possible final product. We are sincerely indebted to him.

VICTOR VIFQUAIN:
A BRIEF BIOGRAPHY

GREAT EVENTS MAKE FOR GREAT MEN, AND EXCEPTIONAL CIRCUMSTANCES call forth colorful, energetic individuals to make their contributions as leaders. Such was the case with Victor Vifquain and his participation in the American Civil War.[1]

A soldier by temperament and profession, Vifquain was recognized for bravery in several major campaigns, where he rose from private to brevet brigadier general and received the Medal of Honor. He was also instrumental in one of the most intriguing behind-the-scenes events of the war: a plot to kidnap the president of the Confederate States of America, Jefferson Davis.

Following the war Vifquain played an important part in the transition of the Nebraska Territory to statehood. A leader in the state Democratic Party, he published a major newspaper, served as the state's adjutant general, held U.S. diplomatic posts, and led the 3rd Nebraska Regiment to Cuba during the Spanish-American War. Only a multifaceted man—pioneer, patriot, and statesman—could have packed so many accomplishments into one lifetime.

On May 20, 1836—a quarter-century before Confederate batteries fired on Fort Sumter to begin the Civil War—Jean-Baptiste Victor Vifquain was born of French parents in Brussels, Belgium.[2] He was called Victor to distinguish his name from that of his father, Jean-Baptiste Joseph Vifquain, a highly decorated veteran of Napoleon's army and a renowned French engineer.

The elder Vifquain's military career began in 1804, when he enlisted at the age of sixteen in Napoleon's cavalry. He served on many fronts and was decorated by Napoleon as a knight of the Legion of Honor for acts of bravery. In 1812, he was designated an officer of the Legion of Honor as a lieutenant colonel of cavalry.[3]

After the Napoleonic Wars, Jean entered the École Polytechnique de Paris (Polytechnical School of Paris), from which he graduated with honors as an engineer. To him are owed the boulevards of Brussels, the canals of Antoing at Pommeroeul and of Charleroi at Brussels, and the first iron bridge on the European continent. This engineering pioneer is also credited with designing the Belgian railroad system, the world's first integrated rail network.[4]

Young Victor Vifquain studied for admission to Belgium's École Impériale Polytechnique (Imperial Polytechnical School) to prepare for a naval career. His father, however, opposed this course and allowed the sixteen-year-old boy to travel to the United States with a friend. Victor returned to Belgium in 1854, most likely called home when his father's health deteriorated. Shortly thereafter he enrolled in the École Militaire Belge (Belgian Military School) and graduated in 1856 as a second lieutenant of cavalry.

But with memories of the journey to America still fresh in his mind, Vifquain resigned his commission in May 1857 and set out on his second trip across the Atlantic.[5] He arrived in New York and then headed west, stopping at Round Hill (Cooper County), Missouri, to see a young woman, Caroline Veulemans, whom he had met three years earlier on his first American visit.

One of seven children of Belgian immigrants, Caroline was born near Natchitoches, Louisiana, on May 20, 1838, two years to the day after Victor's birth. In 1840 the Veulemans family moved north to Missouri, where Caroline's father became a successful livestock farmer. On September 1, 1857, Victor Vifquain and Caroline Veulemans were married at Tipton, Missouri.

In the spring of 1858 the couple traveled to the Nebraska Territory and settled in what is now Saline County, a mile and a half above the forks of the Big Blue River. The nearest town was Nebraska City, seventy-five miles to the east. For nearly a year the Vifquains were the only settlers in the area. They came in contact with the Sioux, Kiowa, and Pawnee, as well as with pioneers going farther west.[6] The old freight road, or cut-off to the California Trail, went past their home in the earliest days, and the same route was later chosen for the road to Pikes Peak, Colorado. After a bridge was built across the Big Blue River in 1861, many caravans of travelers passed their way.

In time Vifquain combined farming with a modest cattle-raising venture. He visited Brussels in June 1859 for his sister's wedding, and his own family grew with the birth of a son in 1859 and another in 1861. Victor and Caroline would eventually have eight children. As the family put down roots on an isolated patch of Nebraska prairie and began looking toward the future, Vifquain began formulating plans to establish a Belgian colony in the rich valley of the Big Blue.

With the coming of the Civil War in April 1861, however, Vifquain's plans and those of an entire nation were changed. Eager to join the fighting and apply his military training to the service of his adopted country, Victor Vifquain prepared to journey far from home and family. He had eloquently stated his feelings less than a year earlier when, admitted as a delegate to the Democratic Territorial Convention in Omaha, he recalled the service given in the American Revolutionary War by France's Marquis de Lafayette. "It is not necessary," he said, "for a Frenchman to promise fidelity to the Stars and Stripes. Lafayette's memory and the French blood spilled for the independence of this beautiful country is a guarantee of it."[7]

Instead of waiting for a local regiment to be formed, Vifquain went east to New York in July 1861, where he expected to find many fellow Frenchmen. He began making acquaintances and studied the recruiting handbills of several regiments before enlisting as a private in the 53rd New York Volunteer Infantry.[8] Organized by Colonel Lionel Jobert d'Epineuil, the 53rd was made up principally of Frenchmen and Franco-Americans, recruited in New York and other Northern states. The nucleus of the unit was drawn primarily from the French-speaking population of Brooklyn. Dressed in the fancy uniforms of the French Zouave soldiers who had fought against indigenous peoples in Algeria, the soldiers of the 53rd New York soon became known as d'Epineuil's Zouaves.[9]

Vifquain was a leader from the start as he was called on to help drill his fellow recruits. In October, he was made adjutant of d'Epineuil's Zouaves at the rank of first lieutenant.[10] As Vifquain prepared for war, his duties as adjutant, such as handling correspondence, keeping records, and distributing orders for his commanding officer, familiarized him as well with the administrative side of military life. During this period, Vifquain's closest friends were two other young French officers of promise and high ambition: Captain Alfred Cipriani, who commanded Company F, and Lieutenant Armond Duclos.[11]

The 53rd left New York on November 18, 1861, going first to Washington, D.C., and then to Annapolis, Maryland. During the first week of January 1862, the regiment left Annapolis aboard the steamboat *John Truck* to join Brigadier General Ambrose E. Burnside's amphibious expedition against the North Carolina coast. But the vessel ran aground in the shallows of Chesapeake Bay near the mouth of a river.

Some of the men stranded on the steamboat were struck with gambling fever. Lieutenant Henry Cocheu wrote in his diary (misspelling both Duclos and Cipriani) that on the rainy night of January 9 the "Col. gambled all night in cabin. Dufloo, Ciprianni, Major, Vifquain & co. kept him company."

The steamboat, freed after several days, eventually made its way down to the North Carolina coast and anchored offshore in a storm. The gambling continued. Cocheu notes in his diary for January 24: "Most of the officers have been gambling every day and night (mostly all night) for a week, the Col. lost all. Poor Ciprianni sold his boots, then his overcoat—his sword belts & c., lost all."[12]

The 53rd never saw combat. The *John Truck*, riding too deep in the water to move closer to land, was ordered back up the coast. The boat and its cargo of dispirited soldiers finally anchored at their starting point, Annapolis, after more than a month of fruitless voyaging.

The 53rd turned out to be a hard-luck outfit, plagued by discipline problems and desertions. The extent of dissension within the regiment became evident in a case involving Cipriani. On February 28, 1862, the regimental surgeon, Henry John Phillips, wrote to Colonel d'Epineuil, complaining bitterly about the young French captain: "I have the honor to inform you that I have caused Capt. Cipriani to be placed under arrest, awaiting the decision of a Court Martial . . . for having insulted me most grossly, not only as his superior officer, but also as a Gentleman. . . ."

Cipriani sat through the lengthy proceedings of a general court-martial, accused of using "highly blasphemous and improper language" toward Phillips in the "presence of an officer and nearly all the Hospital Attendants in the Kitchen of the Hospital."

According to Phillips's testimony, an angry Cipriani, speaking in French, called the surgeon a coward and "only a Dr. and nothing more. . . ." When Phillips arrested Cipriani, he "refused positively to go under arrest" and yelled that he "did not care a damn" for the surgeon's orders.

D'Epineuil weighed in on Cipriani's side, writing on March 1, 1862, to Brigadier General John Porter Hatch:

> I have the honor to forward you enclosed the documents & charges relating to the quarrel between my first surgeon & Capt. Cipriani. I feel it is my duty to say that I think that Doctor Phillips is & has always been very much [prejudiced] against Cipriani & that the latter being a very good & young officer if the matter could be privately settled it would be a benefit for the good of [the] service and the country.[13]

With too many internal problems and dissension to overcome, the decision was made to disband the regiment. The 53rd New York Volunteer Infantry and its men were mustered out on March 21, 1862, after a disappointingly short period of service.[14]

Like his friends and fellow officers, Cipriani and Duclos, Vifquain's hopes of winning military distinction were dashed by the decision to disband the 53rd. Suddenly cast as ex-soldiers of the United States, they were eager for a new mission. And they were motivated by a desire to retrieve a name for the 53rd after its disgrace in being mustered out.

The focus of their efforts turned in the spring of 1862 from the battlefield to an entirely different sort of wartime endeavor. Vifquain and his companions decided to make their way into the heart of enemy territory. Their destination was the Confederate capital at Richmond, Virginia, and their objective was nothing less than the capture of Jefferson Davis. It is this adventure that Vifquain chronicles in the pages of this book.

The plan was set in motion late in March with a meeting in Washington, D.C., of Vifquain, Cipriani, Duclos, and a man they had met at the French ministry, Viscount Maurice de Beaumont, cousin of the secretary of the French legation in Washington as well as a cousin of Prince Camille Armand de Polignac, then a brigadier general in the Confederate Army. Beaumont had secured letters of introduction from the French minister in Washington to the French consuls general in Richmond and New Orleans, setting forth his family connections.

The four young men took rooms at the National Hotel in Washington, where the basic strategy for their mission unfolded. Perhaps over glasses of *vin rouge*, the friends devised a course of action thrilling in its audacity. In the guise of Frenchmen simply traveling about the land, they would go to Richmond and seek an opportunity to abduct the Confeder-acy's president.

Throughout they saw themselves as the bold adventurers of the Alexandre Dumas novel *The Three Musketeers*, with Vifquain as the Gas-con soldier of fortune D'Artagnan, fighting alongside Athos (Cipriani), Porthos (Duclos), and Aramis (Beaumont). These names from the Dumas classic are the ones that Vifquain uses in telling his story.

As related by Vifquain, the latter-day musketeers set out from Wash-ington on March 30, 1862, to capture Jefferson Davis. Their first stop was Alexandria, Virginia, where they registered at the Marshall House under their assumed names. On April 2, they took a train to Manassas, where "Porthos" accidentally shot himself through the hand while clean-ing his pistol. The wound was serious enough to force him to return to Washington.

That night the others moved on, and through a series of close calls and extraordinary incidents worthy of the Dumas novel, they made their way to Richmond, capital of the rebellion and home to their quarry. Fending off charges of being spies and horse thieves, the men befriended a Confederate officer, a powerful prison official who found rooms for them and unknowingly expedited their scheme.

Vifquain describes how the Frenchmen learned that President Davis occasionally traveled from Richmond down the James River to Norfolk on a steam tug to inspect the progress of repairs to the ironclad ship *Vir-ginia*. With this intelligence in mind, they hatched their plan. They would somehow commandeer the tug and run it past Norfolk into Fed-eral hands at Fort Monroe on the tip of the Virginia Peninsula.

How the men pursued this scheme—and later how they fought (and romanced) their way back to Washington, D.C., through the battle-torn Shenandoah Valley—is the adventure related in the rest of Vifquain's book. Less than two months after leaving Washington, D.C., on their self-declared mission to change the course of the war, the men were back in the Federal capital and then went their separate ways. For D'Artag-nan—Vifquain—his greatest adventures lay ahead.

In late June 1862, armed with a letter of recommendation from Sec-retary of War Edwin M. Stanton, Vifquain boarded a train for Spring-field, Illinois. A pleasant change from the larger Washington scene, Springfield nevertheless was a bustling city on a wartime footing. As Vifquain entered the town, signs of military preparation were everywhere to be seen: cannon drawn by wagons through the streets, sutlers with their wares, and soldiers drilling along the main thoroughfare. From the distance he heard the sounds of a drum-and-fife brigade playing a spirited marching tune.

Vifquain went immediately to the capitol, where he presented his letters of introduction and offered his services to Governor Richard Yates. The governor had been charged by the secretary of war with forming forty regiments for active service, one of these being the 97th Infantry Regiment. Organized in August and September, the outfit was officially mustered into the service of the United States on September 16, 1862, at Camp Butler, in Springfield.[15]

Impressed no doubt by Vifquain's background and his enthusiasm to serve, Yates appointed him adjutant of the new regiment. The 97th Illinois was dispatched to Memphis, where it became part of the Army of the Tennessee. By the time the regiment arrived on November 27, Lieutenant General Ulysses S. Grant had begun concentrating Union troops for the impending campaign against the Mississippi River bastion of Vicksburg.[16]

During the winter of 1862–63, Vifquain and his regiment took part in Brigadier General William T. Sherman's Yazoo Expedition north of Vicksburg.[17] In early January 1863 the 97th joined the Arkansas Post Expedition, which was sent to reduce this Confederate stronghold about fifty miles up the Arkansas River from its confluence with the Mississippi. During a frontal assault on Fort Hindman at Arkansas Post, the Federals carried the strong defensive position, with the 97th storming the bastion.[18] Vifquain's demonstrated heroism in his first battle quickly earned him a promotion to major in February.[19] During this period, Vifquain also found an opportunity to engage in his father's vocation. On January 28, 1863, he was "assigned to duty as Asst Engineer" and soon confirmed that engineering talent ran in the family.

Describing his major of French heritage, Lieutenant Carlos W. Colby penned in his memoir: "Victor Vifquain was a Frenchman by birth, with a thorough military education, a strict disciplinarian, a hard drill-master, brave but cautious, always ready for a fight; would 'double quick' us for miles to get us into the thickest of it, thereby gaining us the name of 'French racers.'"[20]

Only twelve days after his appointment to major, Vifquain wrote directly to President Abraham Lincoln and proposed a bold plan: "I should most respectively request of our Excellency, a commission to raise a Regiment of blacks." Outlining his military training and experience, Vifquain asked permission to form a regiment of 2,500 men, about twice as large as usual. A regiment of that size, he indicated in his letter, would be "a change and improvement on the field, it giving a long line and consequently a chance to flank at one time any adversary line—this would resemble the French system. . . ."

Vifquain argued that there were enough potential black soldiers in the Memphis area to form a couple of regiments. He closed his letter with his hope "that you will kindly think to my demand, it being my desire, so humble as I am, to do something for my adoptive country. . . ."[21]

President Lincoln's response, if any, is not known. Besides, a new and decisive campaign in the struggle for possession of the Mississippi River was on the horizon and would now occupy Vifquain's energies.

On May 1 and 2, 1863, the 97th Illinois fought with distinction at Port Gibson, Mississippi. Here, amid the dense magnolia forests of Claiborne County, Mississippi, Vifquain led an attack by the regiment against Rebel troops. His aggressive leadership ensured that his regiment was among the first Federals to enter Port Gibson, a vital road intersection south of Vicksburg.[22] Grant's victory at Port Gibson resulted in the turning of Vicksburg's southern flank; the Union Army was now firmly on Mississippi soil.

The Army of the Tennessee now swung northeastward at will through Mississippi to capture the state capital of Jackson and gain Vicksburg's rear. Here, east of Vicksburg, the decisive battle of the Vicksburg campaign was fought at Champion Hill on May 16, 1863. During this clash in Hinds County, Mississippi, the 97th Illinois again played a role in the bitter fighting.[23] Confederate defeat at Champion Hill led to the siege of Vicksburg by Grant's forces, trapping Lieutenant General John C. Pemberton's entire Rebel army.

From late May to early July, Vifquain and his regiment were engaged in the forty-seven-day siege, including Grant's assaults against Vicksburg on May 19 and May 22, which were repulsed with the loss of hundreds of young men from across the North. Pemberton finally surrendered the city on the Fourth of July.[24]

While fighting to capture Vicksburg, Vifquain had another vital matter on his mind. During this period, he was most of all concerned about the welfare of his wife, Caroline, and his two sons back home in Nebraska. The Sioux in Minnesota had risen in bloody revolt against white settlers the previous year, causing panic across the West and launching retaliatory strikes along the northwestern frontier.[25] The day after Vicksburg's surrender, Vifquain wrote a curt letter to his superior that left no room for disagreement: "Sir, I have made application[s] for leave of absence, and [they have] been refused to me or either postponed, until the fall of Vicksburg. Now, that the greatest of victorys [*sic*]is achieved by the fall of that city, I reiterate my demand. I require a twenty days leave of absence, to settle matters of interest to my family at home; the delay of which, might be a severe loss to their future."[26] He obtained his twenty-day leave of absence and returned to Tipton, Missouri, where his family evidently had moved to live with his in-laws because of the Sioux scare.

Making life more difficult for Vifquain at this time was his deteriorating health as a result of the rigors of the lengthy Vicksburg campaign. In Tipton, a physician evaluated Vifquain and in a July 30, 1863, note to army headquarters stated: "I do hereby certify that by absence of any Army Surgeons in this district that I have carefully examined this officer and find that he is laboring under disease of the liver and kidneys and that in consequence thereby he is in my opinion unfit for duty." The physician recommended an extension of Vifquain's leave by another twenty-five or thirty days.

At the bottom of the physician's letter, Vifquain wrote: "In accordance with army regulations, I certify on honor to the above examination and certificate."[27] The extension was granted. During his leave, Vifquain and Caroline conceived their third child, but in September he was back on military duty in the Deep South. The 97th Illinois was now stationed at Carrollton, Louisiana, just outside New Orleans.

By November 1863, Vifquain was temporarily assigned to the staff of Brigadier General Stephen G. Burbridge as inspector general of the 4th Division, 13th Corps. On November 3 during an engagement at Bayou Carrion Crow, in western Louisiana, Vifquain won new distinction for bravery. With a piece of Union artillery virtually in Confederate hands, he hitched his horse to one side of the gun and ordered men of a Wisconsin regiment to tug with ropes. Mounting his horse, Vifquain raced across the bayou under heavy rebel fire to save the gun. Although his horse was hit, Vifquain was not wounded.[28]

On December 26, 1863, Vifquain was promoted to lieutenant colonel in the 97th Illinois. The regiment next participated in the final stages of Major General Nathaniel Banks's Red River campaign. Lieutenant Colonel Vifquain's regiment skirmished with Rebels in a mean little fight at Morganzia Bend, Louisiana, in May 1864.

But another crisis back home in Nebraska again occupied Vifquain's thoughts. Trouble continued to inflame the northwestern frontier, with the Sioux fighting against the hated "long knives" in blue and the land-hungry settlers. By this time, Vifquain's wife and three children—Victor Emmanuel, Elmer Francis, and Theresa Isabella—had left the Veulemans' home in Missouri and returned to their Nebraska farm on the isolated and unprotected prairies of Saline County.

Vifquain became so concerned over the uncertainty of the situation that he tried to resign so he could return to Nebraska to fight the Sioux. On September 15, 1864, he wrote an emotional appeal directly to Major General Edward Canby, commander of the Union Military Division of West Mississippi, first noting that "I have made application through the regular channel to be sent on duty in Nebraska, but the same has been disapproved." His letter continued:

> My wife and three children are living on Big Blue NT [the Big Blue River in the Nebraska Territory] and but 25 miles from Pawnee Ranch where some people have been massacred by the Indians. Can a man be easy when he has continually on his mind the sad spectacle of his family murdered, his home destroyed. . . .
>
> It is hard General to think about such a thing, and still that is what I am exposed to. I pray you on my knees, Sir to let me go and fight the Indians and to protect all that is dear to me, my wife and children, or die with them in the attempt.[29]

For whatever reason, Vifquain's plea was either ignored or rejected, or perhaps the Indian threat disappeared for the time being. Lieutenant Colonel Vifquain continued duty with the 97th Illinois. Still to come was the Union assault on Fort Blakely at Mobile, Alabama, where Vifquain would earn his greatest military recognition, the Medal of Honor.

The repossession of Alabama was an important part of Grant's comprehensive campaign for the winter and spring of 1865. At length, after Sherman had finished his triumphal march through Georgia and Major General George H. Thomas had decimated General John B. Hood's army in middle Tennessee, Grant decided to move on Mobile. General Canby was assigned to lead the Union expedition against Mobile, a strategic seaport at the mouth of the Mobile River and on the northwestern shore of Mobile Bay.

Garrisoned by 10,000 troops and 300 guns, Mobile defied direct attack. Canby determined to flank it by a movement of the main army up the eastern shore of the bay and, in concert with the navy, to seize the fortifications on the islands and the mainland at the head of the bay. Meanwhile, Major General Frederick Steele on March 20 began an advance northward from Pensacola, Florida, across the swamps of Florida and Alabama, with the objective of taking Mobile from the north.

The 97th Illinois became part of Steele's force. After a difficult twelve-day march, Steele's troops approached the rebel outposts at Fort Blakely. There, ten miles north of Mobile, the Confederates had constructed a defense stretching three miles from a bluff on the river to high ground. Cannons guarded every avenue of approach.[30] With the fall of Spanish Fort at the head of Mobile Bay on April 8, Canby massed his entire force of 45,000 opposite Fort Blakely. In the fading light of late afternoon on April 9, Canby prepared to launch the assault on Fort Blakely and its 3,500 defenders in the last great infantry attack of the war.

By any measure, Fort Blakely was formidable. The fort consisted of nine strong redoubts along the three-mile defensive line. The most powerful sector anchoring the fort's defense was the massive earthwork on the left center known as Redoubt No. 4. The lengthy assault formations of the 2nd Brigade of the 2nd Division, 13th Corps, led by Major General Christopher Columbus Andrews, were now poised before Redoubt No. 4. And among the 2nd Brigade's regiments ready for battle was the 97th Illinois, now under command of Lieutenant Colonel Vifquain.

This was no ordinary challenge for Vifquain and his regiment. Redoubt No. 4 was held by one of the elite combat units of the Confederacy, the First Missouri Confederate Brigade, under command of Brigadier General Francis Marion Cockrell. In terms of both the strength and the quality of the defense, Redoubt No. 4 constituted a daunting objective for Vifquain's men and the other Union soldiers.

On Sunday, April 9, 1865—the last day of the Civil War in the east, as Robert E. Lee surrendered his legendary Army of Northern Virginia to U.S. Grant—Vifquain received instructions to deploy the men of his regiment as skirmishers and to charge the enemy at 5:30 P.M. As dark clouds rolled up from the west and the low rumble of distant thunder was heard, Vifquain, sword drawn and elevated, gave the command: "Forward, Ninety-Seventh! Charge!"[31]

Vifquain and his regiment sprang forward with loud cheers, attacking on the run. They were greeted with a shower of bullets, and before they had progressed twenty yards, several men fell. The 97th under Vifquain reached Redoubt No. 4 and poured across the deep ditch, up the parapet, and then into the fort with shouts of victory. A courageous Illinois color-bearer placed the banner of the 97th Infantry on the parapet, while the Rebels fought back with bayonets and musket butts in hand-to-hand fighting.

Vifquain described the bloody fighting, when "my flag waved on the rebel works: the enemy making a most terrible resistance . . . the regiment was followed very closely by the balance of the brigade, but were not surpassed, although we opened the way." Superior numbers proved decisive, and a surrounded General Cockrell surrendered the blue headquarters flag of Major General Samuel G. French's division, which he now commanded.

Amid a final flurry of combat, Vifquain captured the battle flag of the First Missouri Confederate Brigade. In his battle report of April 10, Vifquain wrote that "the affair was brilliant and a complete success. My regiment captured 1 battle-flag, 1 headquarters flag (French's division), and another battle-flag (Missouri brigade, General Cockrell's)."[32]

To the 97th, whose men slept in the captured fort that night, came words of praise from Generals Canby and Andrews, the latter calling them some of the best young men of the West, proud and gallant in character.[33]

A report on April 11 from Andrews to Brigadier General Lorenzo Thomas, adjutant general of the Union army, praised "Lieutenant Colonel Victor Vifquain, Commanding 97th Regiment Illinois Infantry (to be colonel by brevet) for the noble and gallant manner in which he led his regiment in advance in the charge on the enemy's fortifications at Blakeley [sic] on the 9th instant, and for his general efficiency and earnestness as a regimental commander, and having a regiment of superior discipline."[34]

Vifquain's performance at Fort Blakely later earned him promotion to brevet brigadier general "for gallant and meritorious service" and the Medal of Honor, which he received June 8, 1865.[35] Not yet thirty years of age, Vifquain became the first Nebraskan to be awarded the Medal of Honor.

From Mobile, Colonel Vifquain and his Illinois regiment traveled north up the Alabama River by steamboat to Cahaba, Alabama, on May 1, 1865, with a new assignment. Vifquain was directed to set up an ambush at Marion Junction on the Cahaba, Marion & Greensboro Railroad, about halfway between Montgomery, Alabama, and Meridian, Mississippi. Interestingly, his mission was to intercept a train reportedly carrying Jefferson Davis in flight from a fallen Richmond to rally the Confederate faithful in the trans-Mississippi region.[36] Once again Vifquain was planning to capture the chief executive of the Confederacy.

Vifquain and his best horsemen, on captured Confederate cavalry mounts, rode off from Cahaba before dawn on May 3 for Marion Junction, some fifteen miles away. Two miles from Marion Junction, they were ambushed by the local Dallas County militia, which they drove back through the town after a sharp skirmish. Vifquain and his troops then captured Marion Junction, burned supplies at the depot, and tore up the railroad track. But President Davis was not aboard the train. He would be captured a week later, to the east in Georgia.[37]

The 97th Illinois returned to Mobile on May 12 and was reassigned to Galveston, Texas. With the French now occupying Mexico under Maximilian and the trans-Mississippi Rebels yet to surrender, President Lincoln decided to dispatch troops to the Mexico-Texas border to uphold the Monroe Doctrine and to force diehard Southerners to capitulate. Vifquain was appointed as a commissioner to receive the parole of the last Confederates to surrender, the forces under Lieutenant General Edmund Kirby Smith, at Natchitoches, Louisiana, on May 26, 1865.[38] Vifquain's regiment then moved to Brownsville, Texas, on the Rio Grande, prepared to battle French forces in Mexico. No fighting was needed, however, and in late July Vifquain and his veteran Illinois soldiers were mustered out of service at Galveston. They returned to Springfield, Illinois, on August 19 after three years of arduous service across the South. A few days later, Vifquain bade an emotional good-bye in a farewell speech to his regiment:

> Farewell men of the 97th Illinois! Peace has broken the ties that for three long years have united us together. The moment to separate has arrived. Our task is done: the honor of our country is vindicated. Our glorious Union has been preserved intact and the struggle is ended.
>
> Of all that is dear to our hearts, a soldier's friendship, contracted in continual campaigns, and maintained in the fearful uproar of battle, and in solemn quiet by the bivouac fire, is the dearest and most devoted of friendships. It is so, for God has made it so as a compensation for the many trials that you have endured. . . .
>
> To think that I never more will see you in line of battle, with the stars and stripes waving their glorious folds over you. To think that the 97th will never more be together on the march, in camp or in battle. To think that I nevermore will have a right to say "Fall in 97th!" To think that I will never more have the honor to lead you in battle, is for me a very sad thought.
>
> Still I am happy to return you to your home; happy to think that your wives and children, your parents and your friends will soon

press you to their hearts and hear from your own lips the terrible "History of the Rebellion."

I am grieved to part with you, and still I am happy to return to your Prairie State, four hundred of the nine hundred braves who left their homes and all that was dear to them, to fight the battles of their country. Only four hundred! Five hundred comrades left behind, sleeping the sleep that knows no waking. . . .

Farewell again 97th Illinois! . . . Farewell, God bless you all.[39]

The end of the Civil War brought new challenges for Vifquain, after he returned to his Nebraska home. Not long after the war, he joined the Fenian Movement, enlisting in the struggle to free Ireland from British rule. As demonstrated throughout his adventurous life, Vifquain was in many ways a soldier of fortune, but for the cause of human freedom rather than for personal gain. With a few other Frenchmen, he traveled in 1867 to Ireland, where he served as an adjutant in the Fenian resistance to the British. He narrowly escaped capture before returning to the United States later that year.[40]

Back home, Vifquain directed his efforts toward dealing with various issues in Nebraska. He also helped to develop the state, serving as a surveyor, land appraiser, and pathfinder for settlers in the Republican River Valley. He helped establish a town in Harlan County, along the Nebraska-Kansas border. Not surprisingly, he selected a French name for the new community: Orleans. And he led a party of Frenchmen to Chase County in western Nebraska along the Colorado border, where they planned to establish a large settlement on Frenchman's Fork.

Vifquain entered the political arena again, running unsuccessfully as a Democratic candidate for Congress to represent the fourth District. He was elected to the state constitutional convention in 1871, representing Saline County. As a Democrat, he formed close ties with fellow Nebraskan William Jennings Bryan, who would rise to national prominence.

Vifquain became a leading publisher, establishing the *Daily State Democrat* in Lincoln, Nebraska. As editor he championed the causes of the common man, while opposing the power of state monopolies. The diplomatic world came next as he earned an appointment from President Grover Cleveland to head the American consulate in Barranquilla, Colombia. For his work in helping Chinese merchants find relief from a government-sanctioned monopoly in Colombia, he was awarded the

Order of the Double Dragon by the emperor of China. He also held diplomatic posts in Panama. And in the early 1890s he served as adjutant general of Nebraska.

Not surprisingly, Vifquain supported the cause of Cuban revolutionaries in their struggle for independence from Spain. As early as February 1870, he invoked an analogy from the American Revolutionary War that had much meaning for him: "The hearts of all Americans beat with admiration and love for the Frenchmen who came across the Atlantic to help Washington in his great deeds. We owe it to these men, to our good fortune, and to our independence, to land in Cuba and help the patriots force the Spanish to stack arms and retire."[41]

The Spanish-American War erupted with the explosion of the battleship *Maine* in Havana Harbor, Cuba, on February 15, 1898. In mid-July, at the age of sixty-two, Vifquain joined the 3rd Nebraska Regiment. He was once again a lieutenant colonel in a blue uniform.

By December 1898, Vifquain advanced to regimental command, earning the rank of full colonel. With high hopes, he led his 3rd Nebraska to Cuba, but arrived too late to join in the successful nationalist struggle.[42] Vifquain and his soldiers from the prairies of Nebraska were there to watch the lowering of the Spanish flag and the raising of the Stars and Stripes over Morro Castle, which guarded the eastern side of the entrance to Havana Harbor.

Vifquain returned to his civilian pursuits, including writing his memoirs of the 1862 attempt to kidnap Jefferson Davis. As his health began to fail and he could see the end approaching, he told a friend: "The old tent is campaign-worn, it will scarce longer protect from winter's storm, but the Good commander will provide another, already pitched on the Eternal camping ground."[43] After a full and eventful life, the Frenchman who loved America with a passion and fought to preserve freedom for Americans and non-Americans alike died in Lincoln on January 7, 1904, at the age of sixty-seven.

Vifquain was honored with a formal military funeral ceremony. The governor, veterans' groups, civic organizations, and a National Guard escort joined his family near the capitol and, led by a military band, marched to the Vifquain residence. Vifquain's horse walked with empty saddle and boots reversed in stirrups. After the funeral mass at St. Theresa's Cathedral, Vifquain was laid to rest in Calvary Cemetery.

An exceptional man and a born soldier, Victor Vifquain displayed throughout his life an adventurous spirit, boldness under pressure, and a large capacity for leadership. In his character he combined the seemingly irreconcilable traits of the level-headed businessman and practical politician with those of the visionary and romantic man of action. These were qualities that served him well both on and off the battlefield. In the expanding American republic far from his native homeland, Vifquain had found his destiny.

Link from a Broken Chain:
Historic Reminiscences of the Civil War Relating
to an Attempt to Kidnap Jefferson Davis

To the memory of my companions in arms
who have fallen upon the fields of battle;
To that of those who have fallen since;
To their widows;
To their orphans;
I dedicate these few pages as a testimonial
of my very highest regards and respect.

Victor Vifquain
Lincoln, Nebraska
October 21, 1901

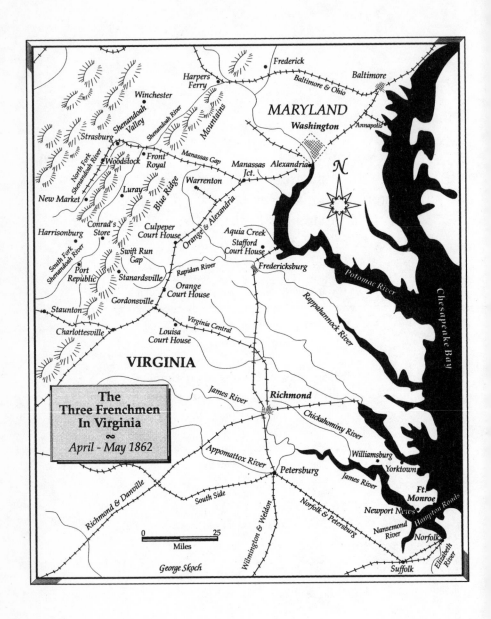

CHAPTER 1

In Washington

IT WAS ON THE 24TH DAY OF MAY, 1861, THAT COLONEL ELMER Ellsworth was shot in Alexandria, Virginia, after having pulled down the Confederate flag from the Marshall House. His death was ever so much deplored, for he was a young and dashing officer, full of promise; it sent a thrill of hatred through the patriotic hearts of the nation; and it found an avenger even before his blood had ceased to flow. James Jackson, the landlord of the Marshall House, expiated his crime right then and there, pierced through the breast with a bayonet, as well as shot through the body, by Francis E. Brownell, one of Ellsworth's men, and the two bodies laid closely together, mixing their flowing blood upon the upper landing of the Marshall House. All this occurred in an old inn of quiet repute in one of the oldest towns of the country.[1]

A great many people visited the historic spot, and it was just about one year afterwards that I found myself doing the same thing.[2] After I had viewed the fatal place, I went to the office and looked over the hotel register. The first entry was made January 1, 1861. While looking over the pages I found the names of many Confederate celebrities who had quartered there. I also found the names of Federal chieftans who in turn had lodged within ints walls. No hostelry of the United States can boast of having the historical seal stamped upon it as this quaint old hostelry had.

While turning over the leaves, and towards the last page of the book, I struck the names Athos, Porthos, Aramis, and D'Artagnan, with residence "Paris," all written by the same hand. My surprise was great, and so was my curiosity. Was it a joke on the part of some wag, I asked the landlord; he knew nothing except that the gentlemen had paid their bills. Evidently the landlord was not a reading man and had no idea whatever of the elder Dumas's masterpiece.[3] I looked at the date of the registry, and if I remember rightly, it was April 1, 1862, only a few weeks before my advent there. I returned to Washington considerably perplexed.

A few weeks afterwards, in early June, while at dinner with General James S. Wadsworth,—then provost marshal general for the District of Columbia,[4] and who was killed two years later while in command of a division of the Army of the Potomac,—I told him about the names I had found upon the register of the Marshall House.

"By George," said he, "you are real lucky; three of them just reported to me a few days ago with dispatches from General Shields,[5] at Front Royal, on their return from a trip to Richmond, where they had gone on their own volition for the purpose of doing with Jeff Davis what Dumas's heroes are said to have done with General Monk, kidnap and bring him here. They failed, however, as might have been expected; they were arrested and came near being hanged as spies and horse thieves. They escaped from the Rebel lines just in time to tell General Banks that Stonewall Jackson[6] was coming; came near being recaptured in a cavalry engagement of Banks's rear guard with the advance of Jackson near Strasburg; and are now at the National Hotel on Pennsylvania Avenue.[7] They dined with me day before yesterday, and I was greatly surprised to see refined and young gentlemen as they are,—you might call them boys,— undertake such an unheard-of achievement. It is the most foolish, daring, and reckless escapade I ever heard of. All three are French, well born, and have their entrées at the French legation."

"What a pity they did not succeed."

"Yes, if they had succeeded they would have accomplished a great feat; a feat that would have made them forever famous in the history of the world. The leader, whose name I guess is D'Artagnan, told me that after they had become convinced that the kidnapping of Jeff Davis was impossible they discussed the propriety of killing him, a thing which they had several times the opportunity of doing. But they concluded that his death and theirs would not end the war any sooner, and for that reason gave it up. And they were right."

So spoke General Wadsworth. My curiosity to see these young men was greater than ever, and I told the general of my determination to see them. He told me that General Ward B. Bennett of proud Mexican fame, took a great interest in them, particularly one of them, owing to having been the guest of the latter's father while in Paris a few years previous, and he advised me to secure a letter of introduction from him to them, as the young men were rather particular, even though reckless to folly.[8]

And so I did, for I was well acquainted with General Burnett, who, the year previous had been surveyor general for Kansas and Nebraska, with headquarters at Nebraska City.

The very next day I repaired to the National Hotel and sent up my card. I was requested to come up, and was taken to room no. 87, but before reaching it I heard some exquisite singing from *Rigoletto*. I had heard the best of singers sing the same song, but this voice seemed to surpass any I had ever heard before, and great was my surprise after the waiter had knocked at the door to hear the same voice drop Verdi's enchanting strains, and exclaim in real musketeer style, "*Entrez!*"

I introduced myself, and begged them to read General Burnett's letter, which I presented. The fact that I was French, young, and also a graduate of the same school as they were, but a few years their senior, made things easy from the start. I was asked to take a seat while one of the two occupants of the room read the note; he smiled and introduced himself and his friend. While he read I took notice of the room so far as politeness would allow,—swords here, pistols there, and a magnificent and huge St. Bernard dog under the table, with shaggy mane, his intelligent head resting between his paws, his big black eyes listlessly looking at me.

The one who had read the letter was D'Artagnan, the other Aramis. I inquired for Athos and Porthos, and was told Porthos was in New York. Presently Athos made his appearance, and I was introduced to him by D'Artagnan, who then remarked: "Now please allow me to inform you that the names used by General Wadsworth and General Burnett are our noms de guerre, and that they were given us by the officers of the 53rd Regiment, New York Volunteers, in which, with the exception of Aramis, we served for nearly eight months; they are none of our choosing, and we use them only when occasion requires. [The name D'Artagnan was employed by Victor Vifquain. The name Aramis was used by Maurice de Beaumont, Athos by Alfred Cipriani, and Porthos by Armond Duclos.] You are acquainted with our family names, but we do not desire them spoken in connection with our trip to Richmond, as Washington is full of Rebel sympathizers, and although not afraid of them we do not wish for any trouble right here."

"I was told" said I, "by General Wadsworth of your presence here after I told him that I read such and such a name upon the hotel register at Alexandria and was very anxious to see some of my countrymen. He told me that you did not wish your names publicly connected with the affair, and I promised him that I would not mention them. I am nonetheless very anxious to know some of the particulars of your trip, which I am told was an eventful one, if not successful as to your principal object."

"Yes," said Athos, "it was one of D'Artagnan's fancies, and it well-nigh cost us our lives. We had, however, a fine time; we enjoyed our folly immensely, and we will be enabled in our old age,—if we ever get old, which is very unlikely if D'Artagnan has any other such ideas in store as the one we have just tried,—to judge of our folly and of the providential good luck we had in getting through it safely. I never thought we would, and we were at all times ready for the very worst."

Of course I spoke French with them, but they spoke English fluently; just the slightest accent, enough of it to make their conversation especially agreeable and interesting.

They were indeed young; the three together did not count threescore and ten, and all three were of remarkably good physical appearance. Their manners at once indicated young men of the world. Two of them were graduates of the [Belgian Military School] and had resigned their commissions to take service in the Federal army. The third one, Aramis, was neither more nor less than a viscount, a duke and peer of France when reaching his twenty-fifth year, a cousin of the secretary of the French legation at Washington, and a cousin also of Prince de Polignac, then a brigadier general in Beauregard's army.[9] He was the exquisite singer I had heard, and upon my congratulating him he said: "Please do not mention it; it is one of those things for which I am not in the least responsible."

D'Artagnan and Athos had been captain and adjutant of the 53rd Regiment, New York Volunteers.

"Now then," said Athos, "it would indeed take too long if we were to tell you all of our trip, and you as well as we have not the time just at present to go over the whole of it. I will tell you what we shall do. We kept notes as a matter of course; we shall make a synopsis of the trip and in a few days we will give it to you so as to enable you to produce a completely written photograph of it. It will take us a few days, meanwhile we shall always be glad to see you, and hope to have that pleasure frequently," and I saw them every day.

The following is what I made from the notes furnished me a few days afterwards.

CHAPTER 2

On the Way to Richmond

ONE OF THE NEW YORK REGIMENTS HAD BEEN MUSTERED OUT IN Washington about March 15, 1862, on its return from Hatteras, North Carolina, where it formed a part of General Burnside's expeditionary army.[1] Many of the officers were foreign born, and most of them were greatly disappointed at finding themselves all of a sudden mustered out; none more so than Athos, Porthos, and D'Artagnan. They were boiling over with military ardor.

While visiting at the French legation soon after their muster out, paying their respects to Mr. Mercier, then French minister at Washington,[2] they were introduced to him who became Aramis. The closest of friendship attached the four together almost immediately, and they quartered and roomed together at the National. Whilst there, the young men became great favorites with Senator Hale and his family, stopping at the same place;[3] also with W. G. Penfield, the millionaire gun manufacturer of Connecticut; and with General Banks and Governor Yates of Illinois, all stopping at the National at that time, and the chances were that these influential gentlemen would soon secure new commissions for them. But it was slow work, at least so it seemed to the young men; then too, they would not like to have been separated.

Meanwhile things were not progressing as they should at the front; the contending armies seemed to be playing hide-and-seek. General McClellan had started for the [Virginia] Peninsula, and disconsolate at being left behind, D'Artagnan and his friends decided to take a hand in the play.[4] On their own hook they concluded to go to Richmond,

[Virginia,] and while there, if possible, kidnap [President] Jeff Davis [of the Confederate States of America] and do all the mischief possible to the Confederacy. Bold undertaking to be sure. They were fully aware of the danger of such an expedition, and indeed had little confidence in the success of their scheme; but they were bent on the "frolic" as d'Artagnan expressed it, no matter the consequences, and so they bade good-bye to their friends at the National, telling them that they would be back in a few days, and leaving their baggage at the hotel.

They set out for Alexandria, and registered at the Marshall House under the noms de guerre above mentioned; they were well armed and had good pistols and trusty swords at their belts and plenty of money in their pockets.

It will seem strange that four young men well situated in life would of their own accord risk their lives as they did, but the youth of those days, whether Federal or Rebel, cared no more for life than the members of the Gironde in 1792; enthusiasm was in the air and had become catchy, contagious.[5]

On the second day of April they took a commissary train for Manassas, [Virginia,] where during the afternoon Porthos accidently shot himself through the hand whilst cleaning his pistol. His friends at once decided to return to Washington, but Porthos would not listen to it, and told them that he would go to Richmond alone if they gave up the trip because of his blunder. He begged them to go on, and promised them that as soon as his hand got well he would come to them wherever they might be. A few hours afterwards Porthos left for Washington, thence to New York; the parting had been as that of dear brothers.

The same night Athos and Aramis, under the lead of D'Artagnan, set out for the South, carefully eluding the pickets, and within three miles of Manassas they stopped for a sleep in the brush. They stopped just in time, for soon after they had lain down they heard the clanking of cavalry sabres and the clinking of spurs, as well as the tread of horses on the road.

A patrol, no doubt; whether it was a Federal patrol or a Confederate they never discovered, and in fact did not care. They had cut loose from the world, so to speak, for the time being, recognizing no master, whether Federal or Rebel; owing nothing to anyone; roaming at their own risk and peril, depending upon themselves alone to accomplish what they had determined upon. In fact, they were their own arbiters.

Soon after sunrise the following morning, away they went, just as tourists would, with their blankets strapped over their shoulders, attired in light blue trousers and jacket,—officers' fatigue dress, less the shoulder straps. Had they been among the hills and dales of Switzerland they would not have been more at their ease.

Happy age; happy feeling! The one of youth that doubts nothing, fears nothing. They took meals where they could, paid for them, and went on. Strange to say that in such close proximity to Manassas they failed to meet any soldiers at all. Before night they were well within the enemy's country and stopped at a deserted dwelling house. A negro woman was hailed and told that a good supper and a good breakfast for three were wanted, and that she would be well paid for them. When Lucullus dined with Lucullus, they certainly never ate with better appetites; neither was there more merriment.[6]

While walking along in the afternoon they had found the country almost entirely deserted; hardly anything but negroes, old and decrepit, were to be seen. As they went they inquired for horses, the walking being exceedingly bad; but they did not succeed in finding any. After supper, however, they inquired of the negro woman who attended them, where horses could be found. A place was indicated some two miles away, where there were several horses.[7] She also told them that there were Texas Rangers in the neighborhood. The rangers had a bad reputation in those days which did not improve during the war, so that before going to sleep after the light was extinguished and the doors closed they had their swords and pistols near to their hands.

They slept the sleep of the just; were undisturbed until broad daylight, when the negro servant brought them their breakfast. Having disposed of the same, they once again set out on their tramp, and at once repaired to the place indicated the night before where horses could be found.

D'Artagnan accosted the owner of the premises in a most polite manner while Athos and Aramis quite unconcernedly proceeded towards the barn to make a selection of such steeds as would answer their purpose. The owner informed D'Artagnan that his horses were all farm horses, and could not be spared at present.

"Really," said D'Artagnan, "we are not in need of racehorses, and I am exceedingly sorry that you cannot conveniently spare them; the service of the state requires the horses and we must have them. As a matter of course, you will be paid for them."

The boys in blue and those in gray had no doubt been there before, and the farmer knew that when they wanted anything they wanted it badly, very badly. D'Artagnan and the farmer made their way to the barn, where Athos indicated three horses and inquired their price.

"Two hundred dollars apiece," was the answer.

"With saddles we will give you three hundred dollars in gold for the three; not a cent more."

And in a commanding tone he ordered the negroes who had gathered around to bridle and saddle the horses, which they did.

The farmer was astonished at the freedom of his visitors, but was unable even to protest although inclined to resist. He read extraordinary determination in the appearance of the three young men, and moreover three hundred dollars in gold at that time was more than the horses were worth; he also knew that the horses would be taken away whether he took the money or not, so he took it. No receipt for the money was given, but the negroes had witnessed the payment.

The reason why the farmer refused to give the horses at first was not because he thought it was not money enough; indeed, money was no consideration in the matter so far as he was concerned. He was an intense Rebel, lean, long, and lank, but too cowardly to fight, and in this respect so unlike the men of his state so deservedly proud of their valor.[8]

D'Artagnan had spoken the words, "the service of the state," and the undress uniform of himself and his friends led the Virginian to infer that they were some of Lincoln's hirelings, as the Rebels used to call the Federal soldiers. When the horses were being mounted, our three friends could detect vengeance in the eyes of their former owner, and they were not mistaken, as the future will show.

CHAPTER 3

A Martial Concert

ONCE OFF THE TURNPIKES, AND FREQUENTLY UPON THEM, THE ROADS were almost impassable to everything but pedestrians; hence in the matter of speed not much was gained. Artillery, cavalry, and wagon trains had passed over these not long before, as the Confederates were changing fronts because of General McClellan's advance by the Peninsula instead of by Manassas. Then, too, the spring rains and freshets were on, and the Virginia clay was thoroughly soaked.

The Federal blue was not overliked in that neighborhood, and the farther south D'Artagnan and his friends went, the worse that feeling became. It had once been discussed among them whether it would not be better to dress otherwise, but the want of other clothes first, and then the thought of intimidation second, made them keep on as they were; surely they could not be taken for spies attired as they were. Looks of hatred and words of insult had become almost general, so general indeed that they were no longer heeded unless the rebuke was from some pretty maiden, and our friends were, as might have been expected, gallant.

In the village of Occoquan on a Saturday afternoon they came well-nigh having a serious time. A considerable number of men being on the street, all in citizens' dress, the soldiers being all gone, an attempt was made to arrest them.

"Why don't you allow us to proceed? We are not disturbing you," said D'Artagnan.

"You have no business down here. Go back to Yankeeland."

"We are Frenchmen, and we go where we please and behave as gentlemen should, which is more than you are doing."

"Dismount, or we will pull you off," and a motion was made to rush towards the heads of the horses by the howling mob. But the horses, quick as a flash, were crowded together ready for a jump and a charge, while the pistols were jerked out of their holsters.

"Stand back," said D'Artagnan, "or we will fire!"

The crowd, perhaps numbering twenty, at once receded.

"We are not Yankees; we are Frenchmen, I tell you. Aramis, sing them a song."

He began at once the French anthem, the immortal *Marseillaise* in the purest French, with a voice that at once took possession of the crowd, which remained speechless in silent admiration. D'Artagnan and Athos joined in the chorus, and as they too were possessed of more than ordinary voices—all Frenchmen sing the *Marseillaise* well,—the natives were treated to a martial concert the like of which they had never heard before.

Strange, the effect of music upon the hearts of men! . . .

"You see we are not Yankees, don't you?"

"Give us another!" cried one of the crowd, and Aramis sang another verse.

By this time the pistols were back in the holsters and many women had joined the crowd, entirely captivated by Aramis's voice as well as by the appearance of those three fearless young men who had the temerity to face almost ten times their number. The result was that D'Artagnan and his friends were permitted to proceed, and so they did, although invited to pass the evening and night in the place as the guests of one of the leading men in the village.

Each night the plans for the following day were talked over, and a full understanding had as to what should be said or done in any case of emergency. The road followed was from Manassas southward to Fredericksburg.

Aramis had a letter of introduction to the French consul general at Richmond from the French minister at Washington; also a letter from the same source to the French consul general at New Orleans. Each letter stated the fact that Aramis was the cousin of General Polignac as well as of the secretary of the legation at the Federal capital. These letters were secured upon the advice of Athos and proved of the very greatest value; besides, they were, so to speak, letters of credit, so that cash would never be wanting.

Aramis had told Mr. Mercier that he intended to go west, that he might find his way south to see his cousin Polignac and that if he did, he would of course like to go to Richmond. The French minister had no idea of the purpose his letters were to serve. Aramis could go where he pleased. He had not been a Federal soldier; his only risk was that incidental to the rather turbulent and lawless state of affairs then existing between the lines and frequently within.

D'Artagnan and Athos were, however, differently situated; they had been Federal soldiers, mustered out, it is true, not owing allegiance to the United States, but nevertheless having borne arms for the North against the South, having in their hearts the bitterest of hatred against the slave-holding power and secession. Aramis was one of the same opinion, probably because his two friends were. And so on Sunday the 6th of April at four o'clock, Aquia Creek was reached, near Stafford Court House.[1]

D'Artagnan knew full well the disposition of the [Confederate] troops on the Rappahannock and the Potomac when he left Washington. He knew that Federal troops had occupied Stafford Court House, but had no idea that the same Sunday morning, [Confederate] Colonel F. H. Lee had found his way there. It was a God-send, however, for it virtually furnished them the key to Richmond without the least premeditated thought on their part as to how that place was going to be reached, except by going towards it, evading obstacles, or passing over them as the occasion might require.

CHAPTER 4

Prisoner of Fitzhugh Lee

THE YELLOWISH WATERS OF AQUIA CREEK RAN OVER ITS BANKS WITH A stiff current. The banks were of even height on both sides as though the stream had been canalized; fields extended almost to the ford on the north side where D'Artagnan and his friends were, but on the other side there was a space of some three hundred yards leading up to some bluffs which, of thirty feet or more in height, seemed almost perpendicular. The road southward could be seen from where they entered the ford; it looked like a deep cut in the bluffs, perhaps twenty feet wide. Stafford Court House is located some two miles beyond.

The horses were at once put into the stream, Indian file, after pistols and ammunition had been safely secured to protect them from the water. D'Artagnan went in first, followed by Athos and Aramis.

The stream was some seventy feet wide, fully fifteen feet deep for the greater part of the distance, so that the horses were obliged to swim nearly all the way across. D'Artagnan, who was in the lead, thought he heard the command "Halt!" But he was not sure of it, and could see no one; moreover, there was no turning around to be done at that time, for the current was very swift and the ford narrow; he proceeded without mentioning the matter to his friends.

They soon reached the other side and, dismounting, shook the water out of their boots, wiped off their swords, and replaced ammunition and pistols in their proper places. While doing this D'Artagnan told his friends that he thought he had heard the cry "Halt!" while crossing the ford, and Aramis with a good laugh remarked that it was the very last place in the world to invite gentlemen to stop.

They remounted their horses and proceeded toward the deep cut in the bluffs. When they had gone about half the distance they heard the cry "Halt!" This time there was no mistake, as they could see half a dozen muskets leveled at them from the top of the bluffs, and those muskets were in the hands of men who wore the gray.

"Rebels," said D'Artagnan in an undertone to his friends. "The Federals are gone. What shall we do?"

"Let us get back across the stream and fight them from there," suggested Athos, and back they went at full speed toward the creek.

Before reaching it a volley was fired by the Rebel pickets, and Athos's horse was hit in such a manner as to cause his sudden collapse, disabling him entirely. D'Artagnan and Aramis at once stopped their horses and asked Athos, who had taken a famous header, whether he was hurt. He was not. The horses being of an inferior quality, there was no question as to mounting any one of them double, and it was impossible for our friends to escape on foot, and altogether out of the question to leave Athos alone in the hands of the Rebels. The young men imediately decided to make a stand right there and took their pistols in one hand and their swords in the other, ready for action.

They thought: "If there is only half a dozen of them we have a fighting chance!"

But a troop of cavalry came dashing down the deeply cut road, and resistance was useless. The troop, numbering twenty, stopped at about fifty yards' distance.

D'Artagnan spoke to his friends: "Remember our plans of last night. You are supposed to speak hardly any English; I'll do the talking and you can hear what I say. This is perhaps the easiest way to Richmond."

The officer in command of the cavalry called out: "Surrender!"

D'Artagnan replied: "There is no need of doing so; we are already captured."

"Place your arms on the ground before you, and step back ten paces."

Our friends did as they were bidden, and thought that the officer must be of a suspicious turn of mind, being so very particular. Then half a dozen Rebels approached on horseback, with carbines in hand, and dismounted when they reached the place where the arms were on the ground.

The officer in command approached, saying, "Gentlemen, you are my prisoners."

"Certainly. But as we are Frenchmen, and not Federal soldiers, I would like to know your reason for arresting us."

"You will explain yourself to the colonel. Oblige me by walking forward."

"Oblige us, sir," said D'Artagnan, "by having good care taken of our arms, as we value them very highly; we expect your colonel will order them returned to us."

And so, following a portion of the troop, the remainder behind them, they marched about one mile and a half before reaching the camp of the [First] Virginia Cavalry.[1]

Our friends were certainly in a rather disagreeable predicament, yet one that had not been altogether overlooked even though unexpected. In their consultations at night they had frequently discussed what would have to be done under the present circumstances, and they were prepared. The surrender of three men to twenty-five, with a whole regiment to back these, was not a dishonorable affair. Moreover, they felt satisfied that had Athos's horse not been shot at the moment when they were prepared to re-enter the swollen stream, they would never have surrendered until the last cartridge had been fired. Their bodies were captured, but the spirit within was not. So they marched on, proud and erect, unable to speak together for fear of being understood by some of the Virginians who were close to the rear.

The officer in command, a young lieutenant, dismounted, and, leading his horse by the bridle, he came to our three friends, with whom he engaged in conversation. He spoke some French and took this occasion for practice as he had but few opportunities of doing so. He told them that Colonel Lee spoke French as well as English, and that he would be glad to speak of Paris, from which he had just returned when the war commenced a short year ago.

The camp was soon reached. It was more of a bivouac than a camp; the only tents to be seen were those at headquarters, towards which they were being led. Their arrival caused quite a commotion, and the Rebel soldiers gathered around in groups, sneering and jeering the prisoners, and the cry "French Yankee" was soon all over the camp. It was with difficulty that the escort could keep on moving towards the colonel's tent.

Insult after insult was hurled at the prisoners, and it was with the utmost difficulty that they controlled themselves sufficiently to keep from jumping at the throats of their tormentors.

"Give us our swords," called our D'Artagnan to the crowd, "and we will soon show you who are afraid and who are cowards."

The Frenchmen had never been in such a predicament, insulted by a howling mob of nondescripts, the very sight of whom was enough to make them raging mad, and unable to strike a blow, surrounded as they were by the escort on horseback. However, their misery was soon to end, for by this time the colonel's tent was reached and the escort in front had wheeled off.

A rather tall form moved back the flap of the tent and stepped out, taking in the situation at a glance. He had already been advised that three Frenchmen had been captured near Aquia Creek. Colonel Lee addressed the prisoners in the best of French, saying to them after having ordered his men to stand back:

"Advance, gentlemen; you are not in danger."

"The danger, sir," said Athos, "does not bother us, but the insults of those men do. I cannot see why they raise such a rumpus over us since we never made a remark to offend them."

"The reason why they are angry is because they have learned that you are French, and they imagine that it is almost an act of treason for a Frenchman to be found among the Northern armies."

"Really. I cannot see why a Frenchman should not serve the North."

"And neither do I, sir," said Lee. "But my men are not as well posted as they might be, and they look upon France as their mother country, just as they look upon every Northern man as an abolitionist. But pray come in."

All this on both sides was spoken in French, and was of course lost to the hearing of the surly troopers around. Colonel Lee was of a fine figure, very young,—perhaps twenty-six years of age—some five feet, eleven inches in height, and of physical proportions indicating great strength. He was F. H. Lee, nephew of Robert E. Lee, and a gentleman and soldier to the tips of his fingers; the idol of his men, a single look was enough for them to obey.[2] The three prisoners were of about the size of Lee; if Porthos had been with them they would have had the better of Colonel Lee, for Porthos measured six feet, three inches in his stocking feet, a regular Hercules in strength, with a face as fair to look upon as that of Colonel Lee.

The Colonel's tent was of good size; beautiful furs were everywhere,—on the ground, and on boxes for seats. As soon as they were in the tent Aramis went up to Lee and begged him to read the two letters of introduction which he presented. While reading them, a smile came over his face and he grasped Aramis by the hand on reading that he was the cousin of Polignac.

"Why," said he, "Prince Polignac and I are the warmest of friends; we came from France together about a year ago. He is now with General Sidney Johnston in Misissippi, and we expect to hear of a great battle over there, as the contending armies are getting near together.[3] How long is it since you arrived in the States?"

"Some six weeks only."

"And you, gentlemen?" said he, addressing D'Artagnan and Athos.

"We have been in the country over a year."

"Have you taken service in the Northern army?"

"Yes sir; Athos and myself have. We are, however, mustered out."

"But how do you happen to be in these parts?"

"Why, Colonel," said D'Artagnan, "as you see by those letters, our friend was on his way to see Polignac and as we were disengaged and at leisure, we decided to go with him and travel at our pleasure. We then fell into your advance post and were taken prisoners; we trust that you will release us and allow us to proceed on our journey."

"I certainly shall not keep you in my custody, for we are on the move. But I cannot turn you loose in that way; however, if you will give me your word of honor that you will proceed to Fredericksburg and report to Major General Smith, you will be at liberty to proceed tomorrow morning. As I have no men to spare, you will oblige me greatly by giving me your word of honor; I will rely implicitly upon it, and let you go alone."

This just suited our friends, and they were pleased to give the colonel their promise as requested.

"By the way," said Lee, "I will give you a letter to my uncle [Colonel Lee], who is in Richmond; also one to General Smith which will enable you to communicate with your cousin by telegraph as soon as you reach Fredericksburg."

The young lieutenant in command of the picket which captured the young Frenchmen came in at this time and delivered to the colonel the arms that had been surrendered by the prisoners. He was told to deliver them to their owners, who were indeed glad to get them back, but who, out of a sense of delicacy, asked Colonel Lee to retain them in his charge until they parted from him in the morning. They were accordingly deposited in the rear tent where Colonel Lee was to sleep.

By this time it was dark and candles were lit. Colonel Lee had decided to let the three Frenchmen sleep in the tent where they had been talking, there being enough furs in it to make them comfortable; in fact, he treated them as his guests, and after having indulged in a simple but substantial meal, they had a pleasant chat about Paris and mutual acquaintances over there, not forgetting the balls of the opera and suppers at the Maison Dorée.

During the evening they learned that Lee, with two regiments of cavalry and a section of light artillery, had arrived in the vicinity that morning, the Federal outposts having withdrawn on his approach, falling back on the Potomac. The object of Lee's mission was a reconnaissance north of the Rappahannock, which at the same time was calculated to keep the Federal forces at and about Washington on the *qui vive*.

It was very late in the night before they retired to sleep; taps had long since sounded, and nothing was heard outside except the monotonous and solemn tread of the sentinel near the tent, and occasionally the stirring and martial "Halt! Who comes there?" to which was answered "Friend, with the countersign."

The four, young as they were, had kept, as may well be believed, a highly interesting conversation.

Reveille and boots and saddles in the early morning indicated the moment of parting.[4] They bade the colonel a cordial adieu, which was warmly returned by him, greatly to the surprise of the troopers who had treated our friends so roughly the evening before. The Frenchmen watched the column by four passing them as if in review and disappearing at a brisk step away in the distance. They then realized that they, too, had to start, but in a different direction, and on foot again as they had started from Washington, for their horses were not to be seen anywhere, and had not been seen since they had dismounted after Athos's horse had been shot near the waters of Aquia Creek. But Fredericksburg was only some twenty miles distant, so off they started.

Everything seemed to favor them so far as their reaching Richmond was concerned, but their vicissitudes were soon to commence. The road from Colonel Lee's bivouac to Fredericksburg was, if anything, even worse than the road from Manassas to Aquia Creek, and D'Artagnan and his friends much regretted the loss of their horses, but as the distance was short they determined to walk it, and away they went.

CHAPTER 5

At the Cottage
by the Roadside

"FINE FELLOW, THAT COLONEL LEE," SAID ATHOS. "WHAT A PITY THAT IT is to be our lot perhaps, some day or other, to fight him."

"Yes," said Aramis, "but if that day ever comes we can console ourselves with the fact that his men have insulted us most bitterly, and he is their responsible chief. By Jove! I feel ashamed yet, and will for some time to come, when I think of the reception they gave us when we entered the bivouac. I am sure that if I had had my pistol, some would have died right there."

"Yes, and so would you, and so would we have died."

"Why, surely Athos, you will not try to make me believe that you are afraid of death, will you?"

"No, my dear friend, but to be killed by such a set would be to die in vain; I trust that when we shall be obliged to give up our lives we may thereby accomplish some good."

"Well, perhaps you are right. Nevertheless, if we are in position to meet Lee and his surly troopers, I will not have the least scruple in fighting the crowd. As Lee is perhaps the only gentleman among them, I would prefer to tackle him; then if I were killed I would at least be killed by a man worthy of the task, and vice versa."

"That is all right enough, but when will we have a chance to meet him with a regiment of cavalry at our back? I fear we shall have to wait a long time, inasmuch as we are now traveling in his own country where he has nothing but friends."

"I am in a hurry to get to Richmond to see what we can do there and then to return to Washington as soon as possible. When I get back there I will raise a regiment of cavalry and will make it a point to find Colonel Lee's command somewhere.

"By Jove! I had no very pronounced idea of my feelings as to Rebel or Federal when I arrived in New York, but I was decidedly born to be a Federal it seems, and I pledge myself to do some solid work for the cause or die in the attempt. Indeed, if it were not for the fact that we have given our word of honor to report at Fredericksburg, I would suggest that we immediately return to Washington, and that we and Porthos at once proceed to raise a regiment of cavalry. With him as colonel we would be in shape to meet Lee at any time, for he would have to look up at Porthos as we had to look up to him."

"Yes, Lee is a fine specimen of a man, but Porthos can beat him by several inches any way, and by an extra hundred pounds in the weight of his blows I am sure. But then Porthos would rather be a private than colonel of a regiment where D'Artagnan and ourselves would be his subordinates."

"Good Porthos! I miss him so much."

Meanwhile D'Artagnan had not said a word but was walking along with his friends, deeply engaged in thinking, not paying the least attention to what they were saying. He heard them talk away, but their words had no meaning so far as he was concerned,—his thoughts were altogether upon a different subject.

"What is the matter with D'Artagnan?" asked Aramis. "Has he become deaf and dumb? He has not opened his lips for half an hour. D'Artagnan, what are you thinking about?"

"I? Well, I was thinking of several things. But first of all, Aramis, let me tell you something,—you must put those letters of Mr. Mercier in some place where they cannot be taken away from you. You had better keep one and let Athos or myself have the other. They are too valuable to run any risk at all with them. If we are again arrested as we were yesterday, we might be searched and the letters taken away from us. They are only valuable to ourselves, it is true, but they might get lost all the same."

"Arrested!" exclaimed Aramis. "For God's sake, D'Artagnan, don't speak of being arrested any more. We were just speaking of that while you were dreaming, and we had half made up our minds, Athos and I, to go back to Washington."

"But we gave our word of honor to Colonel Lee to report to General Smith."

"Yes, and that is the only thing that made us change our minds."

"Oh, we will get back to Washington I feel sure, and by the gods you will have all the fighting you want, my dear fellow, before this thing is half over. But just now we are not in position to offer battle, and we must resort to cunning, for the game we are playing is far more dangerous, I assure you, than the storming of a citadel. Please, then, put one letter somewhere about your clothes where it cannot be so easily detected as in your pocket, and tell us where it is; then give one to Athos, and let him hide it also."

"I think," said Athos, "that D'Artagnan's idea is just the thing; let us get in the brush so that no one can see us."

They did so. It took them but little time, and they were soon again on their way. The letter to General Smith and the one to R. E. Lee were of course left in the pocket, as was also the money in their possession.

"We are," said D'Artagnan, "to all intents and purposes, prisoners, and we will be until we have reported to General Smith. What will become of us then I do not know; it depends a great deal upon what kind of a man Smith is. I hardly think that with the letters we have, and the one Aramis has to General Lee, he will keep us long in Fredericksburg. I am inclined to think that he will do with us what Colonel Lee did yesterday,—send us to Richmond to report to somebody there. By that time we must devise means to enable us to become free men once more."

By this time it was near noon, and as their breakfast had been early and poor, the travelers felt hungry, so they decided to stop at the first house for dinner. It was a nice cottage right along the way; the yard was enclosed with a neat and fancy fence, and had beautiful shade trees and beds of flowers. A knock brought a lady to the door, and D'Artagnan respectfully made his wants known. The lady invited them to enter, and they were ushered into a room where an elderly lady and two young misses were sitting, engaged in some needlework.

Our three friends introduced themselves and apologized for their intrusion, and also said that they were on their way to report to General Smith. They were told that the city was only seven or eight miles away, and that if they would wait a little while some dinner would be prepared for them.

There was in the room a piano that was open as though it had been used but a short time since, and during the course of the conversation Aramis asked the young ladies if they were musicians. In the presence of such young men as ours, the girls felt embarrassed, and were at a loss to say just exactly what they wished to say. A kind smile appeared on Aramis's face, and he told them that if they would allow him he would try his hand, and without further ado he proceeded to the piano.

D'Artagnan had seated himself by the window where he could see up the road in the direction whence they had come; Athos had taken a chair near the most elderly of the ladies, whom he thought must be their grandmother, as she was. D'Artagnan always had an eye to business, and he had selected his place so that in case of alarm they would not be taken unaware.

Meanwhile Aramis played a prelude, and the girls watched him and his companions closely. Presently Aramis began to sing one of his sweetest gems, accompanying himself, and the hearts of the girls began to beat faster at once. His voice was not only exquisite and such a one as mortal seldom possesses, but it was also highly cultured; then he had everything that makes man agreeable: elegance, dash, good looks, and that other one thing so telling upon the other sex,—youth, as he was not over twenty-two. Then, too, there was not the least vanity in his nature; what he did was kindly done and with good grace. He was docile without being inquisitive, generous to a fault, and extremely warmhearted. His friends were in most particulars like himself; all three were in the best acceptance "ladies' men." Aramis's friendship for his three friends was a veneration, just as theirs was for him and for each other mutually.

The two elderly ladies were intensely pleased; it could be seen upon their countenances, and by the manner in which they quickly placed their work on the table nearby. The young misses,—girls of sixteen and eighteen respectively,—still held their work in their hands as though unconcerned, but for their lives they could not have made another stitch at the proper place or proceed with their work in any way. Their eyebrows gradually rose, the eyes opening wider and the pupils dilating. They cast furtive glances upon the singer and his companions; that singing was to them a special revelation, and a pleasure in which they were gradually forgetting all else.

Aramis was even surprising his friends. His singing was no new thing to them, and yet in that cozy little parlor his voice seemed to be more perfect than ever before. D'Artagnan, while listening attentively, yet kept his eye upon the highway, and thought to himself: "That voice of Aramis will help us more than letters from ministers and potentates, provided it does not ruin us." He was pessimistic in the extreme, as may be seen. Suddenly he told Aramis in French to quit singing and playing. He saw six or seven men on horseback rushing down the road towards Fredericks-burg at full speed; they were in citizens' dress, and as they passed in front of the house he thought he recognized the man from whom they had bought the horses. It looked as though they were going to stop, but after casting a look at the house and over the yard they proceeded on their way, and D'Artagnan, who was always cool and imperturbable even in the midst of the very greatest dangers, had risen and, addressing the lady who had opened the door, he said: "Madam, you may deem it out of place for the strangers we are to take possession of your parlor, so to speak, and even of your piano, playing and singing even without invitation to do so, but I beg to assure you that we do not intend to intrude or offend."

Aramis and Athos did not know what to make of D'Artagnan's sud-den fit of extreme delicacy, but while he spoke they heard the hoofs of the horses and saw the men passing by at a gallop. Everything was explained to them, then,—D'Artagnan did not wish the singing and playing to attract the attention of the men passing by.

The lady who had been addressed by D'Artagnan answered: "Why, indeed, sir, no apologies are needed unless it be because you have stopped your friend in the midst of that beautiful song he was so kind to sing us. I assure you that, although you are perfect strangers to me and mine, we feel perfectly safe in your company, feeling certain that you are gentle-men, and I beg you to allow your friend at the piano to proceed."

"You are kind indeed, Madam, and we sincerely thank you. Aramis, you may proceed."

Aramis, who had faced D'Artagnan when hailed by him, now turned again and resumed his singing as though nothing at all had taken place. After he had finished he rose and advanced toward the young ladies, probably to ask them to occupy the piano in their turn, when a colored servant appeared, announcing that dinner was ready. The lady who had met our friends at the door arose and asked them to follow her, which they did after excusing themselves to the elder lady and the two grand-daughters, who remained in the parlor.

Later, rising from the table where they had partaken of a substantial meal, D'Artagnan addressed the lady who had attended them there. He really felt embarrassed, and did not know how to mention the matter of pay.

"I know, Madam, that we are at the home of a lady, not at an inn; yet we are strangers and have not the right to put you to all this trouble with-out. . ."

"Please do not say another word on the subject. I am sure that Mother and myself feel very happy in having been able to serve you and your friends. Besides, your friend there has given us intense pleasure with his exquisite singing, the like of which we have never heard before. I will be most happy if ever again you come this way,—which I hope you may,—to remember that you will always be welcome."

"You are very kind, Madam," said Athos, "and we shall surely avail ourselves of the honor of your invitation."

They went to the door accompanied by the two elderly ladies. When they had passed the gate and were once more on the road, they raised their caps and bade their hostesses a last adieu. The young misses had joined their mother at the door.

"Poor young Men!" said the mother. "Federals, no doubt; but what may they be doing in these parts? These are the ones that this cruel and unfortunate war will most likely claim for victims, just as your father and brother were, my darlings."

"Why Mother, you do not think that they are Federals, do you? I am sure they are Frenchmen."

"Yes, they are French evidently, but their dress indicates that they are Federals, and their presence in this part of the country bodes no good to them, for the Confederate pickets are only a few miles away."

CHAPTER 6

In Fredericksburg;
News from Pittsburg Landing

By this time D'Artagnan and his friends were out of sight but not out of mind of the dear ladies in the cottage by the roadside.

"Now," said D'Artagnan, "let us look at our pistols and see that they are ready for work. I am sure that I have seen the man from whom we bought the horses ride by while you were singing and playing. He had with him half a dozen men, two of whom had guns."

"Well, I should think that he ought to be satisfied with the money we paid him," said Aramis.

"Yes, it was money enough by all means. But I am sure that the man has an intense hatred for everything that is Federal, and he means to get even with us if he can, for the unceremonious manner in which we compelled him to sell his horses."

"Too bad, indeed," said Aramis. "But if he means mischief he had better not come within arm's reach of me."

"How far away are the Rebel pickets?" inquired Athos.

"Well, the place at which we took dinner was only eight miles from Fredericksburg, and the pickets must surely be some three miles this side of the river, so that within two hours we shall strike them."

"And what shall we do then?"

"We will tell them that we bring a message from Colonel Lee for General Smith, and we will show them the letter; that will no doubt let us in."

"Aramis," said Athos, "you were in charming voice before dinner."

"Yes, I felt so much at home among those good ladies; they reminded me of my mother and sister now so far away. Of late we have been living like regular old troopers, regardless of all sentiment, looking death in the face all the time, and hardly thinking of those who hold us so dear and who are constantly grieving over our absence."

The appearance of the country indicated that they were nearing the valley of the Rappahannock; the bluffs were becoming more abrupt and the timber more scrubby. On each side of the road there was timber with a dense growth of slender bushes, and this was enclosed by an old-fashioned snake fence, making a regular lane of the highway.

It was perhaps half past three when a noise was heard ahead of them; it sounded like horses.

"Hark!" said D'Artagnan. "Horses coming. Quick, over the fence!"

"Why," said Aramis, "let us face them!"

"But if they are the Virginian and his gang it will be a fight, and however much I would like to slay him, we cannot just now run the risk. I beg of you, Aramis, over the fence!"

"As you wish, dear D'Artagnan."

Over they went, and it was high time. They laid in the bushes with pistols drawn, ready for action in case of emergency. They were willing to avoid a fight, but were prepared for it if necessary. The same gang of men who had passed the cottage by the roadside went by on their way back.

As soon as they were out of hearing, D'Artagnan said: "Now let us go the other way and hurry to reach the pickets. No doubt those fellows went there and asked for three men on horseback, and having received no satisfactory answer, they have set out again to discover our trail."

They hurried along, and within half an hour came upon the Confederate outposts, where they were halted. Having no countersign they simply asked to be conducted to the officer in charge, as they had a letter from [Colonel] Lee for General Smith. They were conducted to the officer; he was a captain of cavalry, who with his company was doing outpost duty.

D'Artagnan gave him all the particulars, told him that they had been arrested by Colonel Lee's command near Stafford Court House the night before, that they had given their word of honor to report to General Smith, and in proof of it showed the letter that they had. It was sealed and addressed: "Maj-Gen. G. Smith, Fredericksburg." Of course the captain did not feel at liberty to break the seal, and therefore placed the three men in the charge of a squad which was to lead them to Fredericksburg.

"Gentlemen," said the captain, "do me the favor to deliver your arms. By the way, it was only a little while ago that some farmer from Prince

William County came here to inquire for three young fellows on horse-back; are you the chaps?"

"Yes, sir, we are the chaps."

"What has become of your horses?"

"One of them was shot by Lee's men; the other two strayed away while we were being arrested."

"Well, the farmer told me that you had stolen the horses."

"The scoundrel! We gave him three hundred dollars in gold for his plugs."

"He also told me that he thought you were spies. Of course I know nothing about all this, and would rather trust you on your looks than I would him, on his. But as you come from the Yankee lines and can have no business here that I know of, as you do not come under a flag of truce, I will be obliged to report matters just as I know them, to the general commanding. The man who was spokesman told me that he had a warrant for your arrest, and he had with him a posse to execute it."

"Very well, Captain," said D'Artagnan. "Do your duty as you understand it. We submit with good grace and are ready to report to General Smith as we promised to do, and we thank you for your courtesy."

"Hello there," cried the captain. "Ten men and a sergeant to escort the prisoners to headquarters."

He sat down and wrote a communication, which he sealed and addressed to Major G. Smith, commanding Confederate forces at Fredericksburg. What the missive contained our friends did not know, but supposed it was the facts such as the captain had them.

"Give horses to these gentlemen and return as soon as possible," ordered the captain. Then to the prisoners he said, "Farewell, gentlemen."

"Farewell, sir," answered our friends.

They set out at a brisk pace and soon crossed the Rappahannock; they were led to the headquarters of the general at the leading hotel of [Fredericksburg]. It was then about sundown. The town was full of soldiers, and a flag at half-mast was floating over the headquarters, yet there seemed to be great glee among the Rebel soldiery regardless of the emblem of mourning. That same evening news had reached the city that Pittsburg Landing, [Tennessee,] had been won by the Confederates, but General A. S. Johnston had been killed.[1]

The hotel used as headquarters was jammed full of officers and sodiers, and it was next to impossible to enter the building. The sergeant in charge of the escort managed to find his way in for the purpose of delivering his message. Meanwhile our friends were a target for all eyes while they were on the street in front of the hotel; but unlike the evening before at Lee's bivouac, they were not subjected to insult. Yet the situation was, as may well be understood, anything but pleasant to them. Their youthful appearance and dignified bearing impressed the crowd favorably; moreover this same crowd had recently learned of victory at Pittsburg Landing, and the hearts of the soldiery were filled with joy and could tolerate the presence of three prisoners who wore the blue without adding insult to injury.

It was about half an hour before the sergeant of the escort returned, and with him came a staff officer, who directed the escort and conducted D'Artagnan and his two companions to another building not over one hundred feet away on the opposite side of the street. When they had reached it they were ordered to dismount and requested to enter a room where the staff officer informed them that it was impossible for the general to attend to them that evening, but that he would look into their case early in the morning.

"Very well, sir," said Athos, "we will have to submit to your commands, I presume."

The room in which they were confined was a comfortable one on the ground floor, with a window facing an alley in the rear. The sentinel at the door covered both window and door.

While waiting in front of the hotel they had heard about "the Yankees being all cut up and on the run" and they had become impressed with the thought that the victory was complete for the Confederate army, and now and then a cheer was heard for General Beauregard.

"Grant is in command over there," said D'Artagnan, "and it is his first defeat. It is too bad. There is one consolation, however; Albert Sidney Johnston is dead, and he was, so at least I have heard well posted men at Washington say, their best man."

"I would much like to know what has become of my cousin Polignac," said Aramis. "I know he is on the staff of Beauregard and must have taken part in the battle. I will have to wait until morning, I presume, before I can show my letter so as to enable me to telegraph him."

"Why not ask the staff officer about Polignac?" asked Athos.

"I did not think about it, but I will ask the sentinel. Look here, my friend," said he, putting his head at the window and addressing the sentinel, "can you tell me whether General Polignac is all right?"

"I do not know. Why do you ask?"

"He is my cousin, and I would like to know." One of the soldiers in the street told Aramis that the particulars of the battle were very meager as yet, and that nothing was known of it except that the Yankees were whipped and Johnston was killed.

It was quite dark by this time, and a regimental band was serenading about headquarters, the music of which could be heard perfectly in the room, and among the pieces that were being played was "Maryland, My Maryland."[2] The music, which is of French origin, was a great favorite of Aramis, so that singing the French words of it, he at once joined in with the band. As the window was open, his sweet voice attracted more attention than the band itself, and the alley became crowded with Rebels, who applauded and cheered vociferously when he had finished and kept up the applause until Aramis came to the window, where he sang "Maryland, My Maryland" in a manner that kept them perfectly spellbound, and thrilled his military audience with enthusiasm; the band even ceased while he sang.

The song finished, he was cheered to the echo, and after closing the window he retired into the room. Presently the staff officer who had conducted the prisoners to their place of abode entered, and with the compliments of General Smith requested the presence of the singer at headquarters to entertain the general.

"Give my thanks to General Smith for his appreciation of my voice, but tell him that I am not in the entertaining business. I say this with all respect to you, sir, and without the least wish for offence to anyone."

The officer, himself a man of the world, at once saw what sort of men the three friends were. He insisted as much as he thought he ought to, and then retired; but before he left, D'Artagnan spoke up and said: "Sir, our friend here is anxious to have news of his cousin, General Polignac, who must have taken part in the battle fought yesterday. Are there any particulars concerning him?"

"No, we have heard nothing about General Polignac, and consequently he may be presumed to be all right."[3]

"I thank you, sir," said Aramis. "I was very anxious to ask you to tell me what you have just told my friend, but as I have been obliged to refuse you to attend at headquarters as you requested, I did not feel at liberty to ask you."

"And that is the reason why I inquired," said D'Artagnan, and the staff officer retired.

The band kept playing until a late hour, but our friends heeded it no longer, and they had quite a talk over the possible events of the morrow.

"The Virginian from whom we bought the horses is liable to give us much trouble," said D'Artagnan, "in case he pushes the accusation of having stolen his horses, against us."

"Yes," said Athos, "But there are three of us here to swear that we paid him three hundred dollars."

"To be sure, but he is a Rebel, and he has with him other Rebels, as we have seen, and the weight of their evidence is against us."

"And what of the negroes, who saw us pay him the money?" asked Aramis.

"They were negroes and slaves. They would not dare to testify against their master even if they were allowed to do so; moreover, they are not here."

"Well," said Aramis, "I will show my letter of introduction to the consul general at Richmond from the minister at Washington, and that will no doubt prove satisfactory."

"Yes, that will have some weight," replied D'Artagnan, "nevertheless the accusation will add more suspicion against us than we really can afford, and besides may cause us delay. We have something else to do than appear before a tribunal under such charges as that infernal Virginian is trumping up against us."

"The fact is," said Athos, "that our position is not overpleasant. It is all very good for us to tell that we are Frenchmen and that we are traveling for pleasure on our way to see General Polignac, but to make them believe it is another thing."

"And yet they have to believe it," said Aramis.

"I wonder," remarked D'Artagnan, "what the effect of the Rebel victory at Pittsburg Landing will have over the operations of the troops here? It will no doubt depend upon the extent of that victory, and if it is as complete as the fellows around here seem to believe it is, they may decide upon an immediate advance on Washington now that they must be aware that General McDowell's corps is alone between them and the Federal capital."[4]

"But what of Richmond, then, with General McClellan coming up on the Peninsula?" said Athos.

"The Rebels can easily get out of Richmond and fall back, but the Federals cannot so readily get away from Washington. Don't you think, Athos, that the capture of Washington would be a more disastrous blow to the Federals than the capture of Richmond would be to the South?"

"I do, decidedly so. But the Rebels could not hold Washington, even if they captured it, while the Federals can hold the Confederate capital and will hold it, I'll warrant you, if they ever get it."

"Why?" asked Aramis.

"Because the North has the resources, while the South has not. We can keep one hundred thousand men in Richmond and not miss them; the South could not maintain that force in Washington. From a military point of view I think it was a mistake on the part of the South to establish their capital at Richmond; it is an element of great weakness."

"Yes," said D'Artagnan, "I have heard Mr. Mercier say the same thing."

"And what of the prestige of such a thing as the capture of Washington?" asked D'Artagnan. "Would it not lead to the recognition of the South by the powers of Europe?"

"No, I think not," said Athos. "God Almighty Himself would not recognize the South, and even though it were recognized it would only add to the determination and the power of the North to crush out the insurrection that has human slavery for object and being."

"Well," said Aramis, "let us wait and see what tomorrow will bring forth. I feel that we will manage to get out of this all right no matter what the consequences of the Federal defeat in the west may be, and when we do get to Richmond that defeat, as well as the troubles we may have in reaching that city, will stimulate us to greater action. Let me tell you one thing,—the first time I see that Virginian, as we saw him today on the road, I will settle my score with him at once and forever."

"So shall I," said D'Artagnan.

"And I," joined in Athos.

Sweet unanimity that bodes no good to the rascal! Luckily for him, however, they were not to meet him right then. He had started from home after securing a warrant for the arrest of our friends, having sworn to the charge of horse stealing and spying, and in hopes of catching his prey before they entered the Rebel lines, but in this he had failed; having lost their trail as has been seen, he arrived at the conclusion that those whom he pursued had taken some other route. As bad a report as possible of the character of D'Artagnan and his friends was made to the captain of the picket, and after that he quietly returned to his home the same way he had come.

Horse thief and spy were indeed names that neither Federal nor Rebel relished, and to be suspected of either one or the other was bad enough; but to be suspected of both was about equivalent to a death warrant.

The street had become quiet after the rejoicing of the evening; the soldiers had returned to their quarters, and our friends had lain down to sleep.

CHAPTER 7

The Field of Battle

THE NEWS OF PITTSBURG LANDING AND THE DEATH OF GENERAL Johnston reached Fredericksburg some twenty-four hours after the memorable events had occurred. In those days the telegraph was not what it is today; moreover the Southern lines, whether of telegraph or of signal, were under the control of the military and only such news was made public as would not create undue excitement. When it was the news of victory, of course publicity was not delayed; but when it was news of a defeat, the announcement was not so soon promulgated. Shiloh was fought and won by the Federals the day after Pittsburg Landing, and yet the people of Richmond never learned of it until the 9th of April, or forty-eight hours after Beauregard had been routed.[1]

Was Pittsburg Landing a victory for the Confederacy? In one sense it was, in the other it was not. It was a victory so far as prestige was concerned; it was not a victory so far as results, and victories should be measured by the latter. The Federal forces were checked in their advance and even repulsed, but that repulse did not take away the advantage they gained by the crossing of the Tennessee River.

The objective point when Sherman, Wallace, and Prentiss crossed the river was Corinth; this was well known by the Confederates.[2] The battle of Pittsburgh Landing,—or to speak more to the point, the first day's fight of the battle of Shiloh,—delayed Grant only one day, and this delay never proved of any benefit to the Rebels; on the contrary it cost them the life of General Johnston. If he had not been killed it is possible, even probable, that a Rebel victory would have been the result even in spite of General Buell's arrival on the evening of the 6th.

Some people criticized General Grant for having crossed the Tennessee before Buell's arrival, but in this they surely err, for it is always a general's duty to cross streams at the very first opportunity so to command both banks. This is always a great advantage. If any criticism at all attaches to General Grant's conduct, it should be for having accepted battle on the left bank before Buell's arrival; he should have contented himself with occupying the left bank with Sherman's and Prentiss's divisions, a thing which would have been easy and perfectly successful, thanks to the gunboats at the landing.

Then again, a great deal of unfair and unjust criticism in refutation was made against General Buell for not having arrived on the morning of the 6th instead of in the evening, and he became the martyred victim of that criticism. The fact is that when General Grant crossed the Tennessee he was under a misconception as to General Johnston's strength, and that is all.

The prestige of the Rebels for the [first] day's operations at Pittsburg Landing was, however, no dishonor to the Federal troops; indeed the valor displayed by Sherman's divisions upon that day will ever stand to the imperishable honor of the western soldiery. Justice has not been rendered to the men who fought on that field, not only against heavy odds but also against a powerful position held by the enemy.

The periodicals have been filled with descriptions of Gettysburg, Antietam, Fredericksburg, Chancellorsville, and other fields, where eastern troops were principally the combatants, and well-merited praise given to the valor of the men thus engaged. But when the facts shall all have been thoroughly sifted, the valor of the Federals at Pittsburg Landing will prove to be even superior to that displayed at Gettysburg.

The latter was a bloody field, to be sure; but look at the numbers engaged, and the time it took to fight the battle. There were nearly 160,000 men engaged [at Gettysburg], and the total loss of all kinds, Rebel and Federal included, during the three days [July 1–3, 1863], is estimated at 50,000, both sides included, or nearly one-third of the effective strength. What of Shiloh? There were about 50,000 men on the field, both sides included, and the losses were fully 22,000, or nearly one-half of the effective strength, and this in a two days' fight only.

Then again look at Champion Hill, [Mississippi, in May 1863], where [General] Pemberton not only had choice of position but a force at least equal to General Grant's, Sherman having been directed towards Jackson, [Mississippi].[3] And still again look at the charges against Vicksburg, [Mississippi,] on the 19th and 22nd days of May [1863].

Why! Terrible as was Gettysburg and great as were the valor and endurance of the Federals there, it becomes insignificant as compared with the valor and endurance of the Federals on those memorable days.

General Grant had no doubt some good reason for insisting that his men, who in numbers were hardly equal to Pemberton's army within Vicksburg, should take that stronghold by storm. Yet he ought to have known that if the army he then had could not make a successful assault on the 19th, that it was beyond all human possibilities for that army to make it at any subsequent day. There never was a better or more effective body of men drawn in line of battle anywhere on the globe than the army that crossed the Mississippi River at Bruinsburg Landing and fought its way to the Rebels' far-famed stronghold. Grant never fought a grander battle than Champion Hill, and Sebastopol itself was not more valiantly defended than Vicksburg.[4]

It is to be hoped that the history of the western fields will some day be written in such a manner as to teach the generation of the present and the generations of the future that all the fighting of the way was not done east of the Alleghenies. Richmond may have been, and was, the last place to fall, but Sherman and his western boys had to march through Georgia and to the sea before it fell. There were no more worlds for the western men to conquer; their task was accomplished. They had marched from Cairo, [Illinois,] to New Orleans, from Natchitoches and Shreveport, [Louisiana,] to Missionary Ridge; they had fought on a hundred different fields until there was no Rebel army worthy of the name left in the Mississippi Valley; no foe worthy of their steel to encounter, and in the grand round-up they were happy to land their eastern brethren the assistance of their valor, and they did so after marches and countermarches, battles and counterbattles, the like of which history had never before put on record.

And while the historian is doing this, let him also teach the reader that the rank and file who fought the battles are also the men who won them, and that to them at least belongs the greatest part of the honor. Generals seldom fight; they plan battles, sometimes; but in the main our battles were fought on the principle of "catch as catch can," and the victory as a rule remained to the best men and to the heaviest battalions. A great chieftain has said: "God is on the side of the heaviest battalions."

In one word, General Grant did not whip the Rebels; the northern men did it. If any man had prestige on the Federal side, that man was Grant; his men had the utmost confidence in him. They loved him, and yet that confidence and love did not lead them over the walls at Vicksburg, nor through the wilderness; their valor and power of endurance alone did that.

The true heroes of the war are to be found in the ranks and not among the generals. The ranks were full of heroes; they marched to victory accompanied by the god of fortune and by the god of war; these were the mystic leaders, and the hero worship of this day should begin where it belongs, or better still, should be set aside altogether, as unworthy a nation of intelligent men and the government of a free people.

CHAPTER 8

In Libby Prison

IT WAS ABOUT NINE O'CLOCK IN THE MORNING WHEN D'ARTAGNAN AND his companions were led to the headquarters and into the presence of General Smith.[1] He received them very coldly, and in a manner which impressed them very poorly with the general's qualifications as a gentleman. He bluntly asked them what they had to say for themselves in answer to the charges preferred against them by the farmer of Prince William County.

"General," said D'Artagnan, "will you allow me to present you this letter?" He presented Colonel Lee's letter in which the latter informed the general that the bearers had given their paroles to report to him. When the letter had been read, D'Artagnan said: "Now, General, we have the honor to report to you in accordance with our paroles and to await your pleasure."

"This letter," said Smith, "does not refer to horse stealing and spying; what have you to say about that?"

"Say! We say that both charges are infamous lies; we say that we are Frenchmen; we say that if it was the undoubted right of Colonel Lee's pickets to arrest us, it is also your duty to release us as soon as you become convinced that we can neither be horse thieves or spies."

"And why could you not be either?"

"Because we are gentleman, and because if we had been what you assume we might be, we never would have kept our paroles."

"Gentlemen! Gentlemen! What proofs can you give me that you are gentlemen?"

"General," said Aramis, "I do not know what you are. It is to be presumed that you are a gentleman, since you are a major general, and we intend to treat you as such. But without being generals we claim to be at least your equals as gentlemen."

"You talk rather loud, young man! Do you known whom you are addressing?"

"I know, sir," said Aramis, "that when you have read this letter of the French ambassador at Washington you will perhaps be convinced of the truth of what we say."

Aramis handed the letter to the general. After reading it he said, "So then you are the cousin of General Polignac?"

"Yes sir, I am the cousin of General *Prince* de Polignac," placing emphasis on the word "Prince."

"And you are the one who sent me word last night that you were not in the entertaining business?"

"I am, sir, and I need not tell you, after the manner in which you have treated us, that I am very glad that I refused to entertain you."

"Very well, sir cousin, that was your right. Meanwhile I will send you all three to General Winder, the provost marshal general at Richmond for trial as horse thieves and spies."[2]

He handed Aramis's letter to the staff officer in attendance, who returned it to the owner.

"General," said Athos, "probably we may be tried, as you say, but we do not fear the result. I am in hopes, sir, that after the trial we may have the pleasure of meeting you again; we shall then meet you on equal footing."

"What, you dare to threaten?"

"No, sir," replied Athos with great dignity; "we never threaten. Gentlemen seldom do; we simply advise you of our desire to meet you again after we have cleared ourselves of the ridiculous as well as infamous charges that are being trumped up against us. That is all, sir."

The general addressed the officer in waiting: "Take those men back to the place where they were; keep them in close confinement. During the day I will prepare a report of their case, and tomorrow morning they will be sent by the early train to Richmond to be turned over to General Winder. I never saw such impudent youngsters."

The general was in a rage. It was perhaps the first time since he had become an officer that he was spoken to by men who dared to acknowledge that their souls were their own. In retiring they all three doffed their caps to the general, with a smile upon their faces, and walked proudly away as men to the manner born, which they were.

The general meant to make such a report of the case as would leave no loopholes for their escape so far as he was concerned.

On the way to their place of confinement Aramis asked the officer who had them in charge whether there was any chance for him to telegraph to Polignac; he was told that it could not be done without the consent of General Smith.

"I would rather die than ask his consent."

"Wait until you get to Richmond, and there surely you will have an opportunity to telegraph as you desire."

"I thank you, sir."

And they were once again incarcerated. Being left to themselves, D'Artagnan said: "Well, we will get to Richmond anyway; but what do you think of General Smith?"

"Think? Why, he is a regular brute," said Aramis, "and I am very glad Athos told him, in his inimitable way, what he has the right to expect when we meet him again after we are free. The fellow takes us for little boys whom he imagines he can scare, but he will learn better."

"Well, I really think that we have in the main been very fortunate. We might have been killed several times since we left Washington, we might have been separated, and yet our only mishaps were at Lee's bivouac and here with that man Smith."

"But, D'Artagnan," said Athos, "don't you think they will give us some trouble in Richmond before we are set at liberty?"

"I think not. Aramis must manage to send a dispatch to Polignac at the very first opportunity, and a simple request from Polignac will, I dare say, set us at liberty. Then we will take our bearings as to Mr. Davis so as to get even with his minions. Moreover the consul general of France will not allow us to be treated like vagabonds, I assure you, and I am told that he is quite a power at the Rebel capital."

"Horse thief and spy!" laughed Aramis. "By Jove, my dear friends, I never knew that our appearance was so bad!"

"But," said D'Artagnan, "I would venture to wager that Smith does not believe a word of those charges himself."

"No, but nevertheless he treated us little better than if he did."

"If he really believed it, we would have been separated and put into places far less comfortable than this."

"On to Richmond!" said Athos. "Well, we are doing our share, and Mr. Greeley ought to feel satisfied, for he has been urging 'On to Richmond!' to everybody, and everybody in this latitude is trying to get there as soon as possible excepting Mr. Greeley himself.[3] If General Smith keeps his word we will reach there tomorrow."

"God grant it," said D'Artagnan.

The aide-de-camp who had called the evening previous with the compliments of General Smith, and who had also conducted our friends to and from headquarters in the morning, made his appearance during the forenoon and said: "Gentlemen, I am instructed to ask your names and some particulars in your case." He seated himself by the table and prepared to write.

D'Artagnan gave their true names, adding, "We were born in Paris and are French citizens. We beg to protest against the arrest we are now undergoing."

"Where were you going when arrested?"

"We were on our way to see General Polignac, my cousin," said Aramis, "and as he is in the service of the Confederate states, we were constrained, to our very great regret, I assure you, to come within the Confederacy to find him."

"Are any of you in the service of the United States?"

"We are not."

"How long since you came to America?"

"Two of us have been in the country for nearly eight months; the other only three months."

"Very well, gentlemen. I thank you. Tomorrow morning you will be sent to Richmond. I wish you good day."

Early next morning they were put in the charge of an officer and two men, on their way to Richmond, where they arrived towards noon. It was a matter of great surprise to D'Artagnan and his friends that no fortifications at all surrounded the Confederate capital.

Owing, they presumed, to the news of [the Confederate defeat at] Shiloh, which had just reached the city, a disaster altogether unexpected, the city was full of excitement and our three friends were at once taken to Libby Prison.[4] It was then one o'clock, April 9, 1862.

CHAPTER 9

On Parole in Richmond

As D'Artagnan and his friends were not soldiers, they were not put with the prisoners of war but were given a room to themselves. It contained six or seven cots, all scrupulously clean, and was situated on the left of the main entrance. General Winder, the provost marshal general, had turned over the case at once to a Captain Alexander, provost marshal for the district of Richmond. This captain was the man who but a short time before had escaped from Fort McHenry, Baltimore, through the assistance of his wife who, when on a visit to her husband, had changed clothes with [him]. The event created quite a sensation, as some readers may remember. He was of French origin and spoke the language to perfection, and it was indeed a happy incident for our friends that their case was intrusted to his care.[1]

The morning after their entrance at Libby, Captain Alexander came to see them. They put their case before him and requested that the French consul general be advised of their desire to see him; they also asked permission to communicate with General Polignac by telegraph, and this was granted. As to the charges made against them, implicating them as horse thieves and spies, they denied them most emphatically, but insisted on as speedy a trial as possible.

The captain told them that he would have them removed to his own office, where they would be more handy to him, and so they went. They were given a room on the second floor right over the office. From a window they could see the sale of slaves in the house just opposite on the ground floor. This was a novel sight to them, a thing of which they had heard but had never seen before, and it proved most shocking to all three. The street being a narrow one they could not only see very well, but could almost hear every word that was spoken in the auction room.

The slave put at auction was standing on a block about two feet high; around stood a set of villainous-looking individuals who, while the auctioneer proclaimed the mortise of his chattel, examined him just as a horse would be examined. They looked at his teeth, felt the muscles of arm and thigh, turned the poor being around to judge of his proportions, and finally made a bid,—a bid for a human soul! The poor black upon that block was truly emblematic of the most disconsolate desolation. The spectacle was even more heartrending when the chattel happened to be a woman. Most of the men standing around as bidders had rawhide whips in their hands.

"A curse upon them!" said Athos. "A cause bolstered up by such a system of inequity is bound to perish, and must perish!"

"And it will perish!" agreed D'Artagnan.

Captain Alexander took a great interest in his prisoners, passing much of his time with them. He enjoyed their company, their conversation, and they in turn took quite a liking to him.

On Sunday the 13th, a dispatch came from General Polignac to Aramis telling him that he had sent word to General Winder in identification of him and requesting that he and his friends be released and allowed to proceed on their journey to see him. This was great news for the three friends, and in celebration of the event they invited Captain Alexander to join them in the destruction of a first-class meal which they had ordered at some neighboring restaurant. The invitation was accepted, and it goes without saying that the dinner was a pleasant one. It was upon this occasion that the captain told of his escape from Fort McHenry, and how he had broken his [ankle] in jumping over the wall.[2]

At the end of the dinner, when the coffee was being sipped and the cigars smoked, Aramis in compliment to his guest sang "My Maryland" in the French dialect. It struck the captain in the very tenderest part of his heart and brought the tears to his eyes. Aramis was in splendid voice, and had succeeded very unconsciously in getting a crowd in the street that blocked all possible circulation, and which, when he had finished the song, cheered him to the echo with the most generous applause.

"Forsooth," said Aramis, "I had forgotten that the windows were open."

"Oh," said Alexander, "there is no harm done; that song always manages to stir up our most patriotic feelings, but when it is sung by a voice such as yours, the like of which I have never heard in Richmond or in the South for the matter of that, then the enthusiasm becomes admiration."

The crowd in the street wanted more, but Aramis asked Alexander to excuse him to them, which he did.

"Your reputation as a singer is made, and the papers tomorrow morning will spread it all over Virginia."

"Yes, and I know how to stop slave-selling hereafter."

"How?"

"I will go to the window and sing and sing until the street is blocked and all business stopped.

"Does that slave-selling disturb you?"

"Yes, indeed," said Athos. It seems to us to be about the very thing that could be seen,—heartless and cruel."

"Well, it is probable that the dispatch sent to General Winder by Polignac will cause your release tomorrow, and thus you will be relieved of the sight. I would give you another room, but this is the only one I have vacant, and in fact the best in the house."

"Dear Captain," said D'Artagnan, "we are just from Europe, and have not and cannot have very pronounced ideas about slavery, but the sights we have seen in that auction room opposite are truly repulsive to human nature. Several times we have been on the point of calling out that they ought to be ashamed of themselves for treating inoffensive blacks as they did. But out of consideration for you, who has been so kind to us, we have refrained."

They remained together until a late hour, and the captain left them, satisfied that all three were perfect gentlemen; they had made a fast friend of him. . . .

Early the following morning an order was sent to Captain Alexander to bring his three prisoners before General Winder, and they reported accordingly.

"Which of you is General Polignac's cousin?" asked Winder.

"I am, General."

"Well, here is a telegram received from him yesterday," and he handed it to Aramis to read.

"After consultation with General Lee," continued Winder, "we have decided to give you the liberty of the city. I will take immediate steps to secure the man who has made charges against you, and when I have him, you will be confronted with him."

"General," said D'Artagnan, "we denounce the charges as infamous."

"Yes, and I am inclined to believe you. Nevertheless, duty compels me to act as I do. Now then, Captain Alexander, you will release these gentlemen and they will report to you daily at such time as you may designate. They will be allowed to stop at such a place as they please, and if, within a reasonable time, the man who accused them does not make his charges good, they will be at liberty to go to New Orleans, where General Polignac is likely to be."

"General," said Aramis, "when we were arrested we had swords and pistols which we think much of, and would like to know if they can be returned to us."

"Yes, they are here and will be returned to you when the thing is over, as I hope it soon will be."

And they retired. Captain Alexander took them to the St. Charles Hotel, where they took rooms. The captain congratulated them and promised to call. He requested them, in accordance with General Winder's instructions, to report to him at his office at such an hour as might be most convenient to them, and he left.[3]

Before doing anything else, the three proceeded to purchase clothes, so as to attract as little attention as possible, their Federal suits being too conspicuous. After having renovated themselves from head to foot they took a stroll and then returned to the hotel, where the landlord himself would not have recognized them when they called for their key, had they not stated the number of the room which had been assigned to them when they registered their names.

Their room was elegant; in fact they had two rooms, one a sleeping room and the other a sitting room or parlor. Having examined their surroundings they came to the conclusion that it would not do to speak too loudly when in consultation on the main questions for which they were in Richmond.

"Moreover," said Aramis, "it is probable that some one will keep an eye more or less upon us until we have been entirely released."

This was a happy day for them and they could hardly realize that they were in Richmond, and to all intents and purposes as free as though they were at the National Hotel in Washington. Then, too, the city was a novel sight to them, so vastly different from what they had been accustomed to. It was but a short time ago that they had been at the Federal capital, and now the Confederate capital presented itself to them, with the same military enthusiasm and bustle predominating in both.

Literally speaking this one might have been called the Gray Capital as the other was the Blue, with the same rush here as over there. Hardly one hundred miles apart,—twin sisters, so to speak, only one year ago, but now separated by an ocean of thought and blood! The pride, the brain, and the heart of Southerners were in Richmond, as the heart, the brain, and the pride of the North were in Washington. . . .

The same martial spirit that animated the youth at Washington city animated also the youth of Richmond, even to a greater degree. Regiments were marching in from all points of the compass almost every day, and were sent towards the Chickahominy [River] to take part in the gigantic struggle that was soon to take place over there.[4] Their appearance upon the streets as they marched by created the most unbounded enthusiasm, and the fair daughters of the South showered a rain of flowers over them.

Of course D'Artagnan and his friends quietly watched all this from their windows, without the least rancor in their hearts, but yet with a desire to meet them in battle array, a thing for the time being they had little likelihood of doing. They knew, however, that all these men could accomplish nothing so far as secession was concerned; they knew that all that mass of humanity would only play the part of "cannon flesh," all of them bound to be destroyed sooner or later, inasmuch as for every man sprung from Southern soil to do battle for the Southern cause, three equally as good men would spring from the loins of the North to do battle for the Union.

The feeling in Richmond against Northern people was, however, much more savage and bitter than the feelings in Washington against Southern people. The vista of ultimate disaster and destruction, the hopelessness of their cause, stared the Southerners in the face from the start.

Our friends, although they were not Northern men, yet had their cause so much at heart that to avoid being obliged to resent insults against the Northern people, concluded to keep themselves as much as possible in their own rooms. It would have given them much joy to meet at any time an even number of Rebels, but an outburst of anger at the hotel where they were would mean a struggle of one against ten, and the dashing to pieces of the purpose for which they had found their way out there.

They even had their meals sent to their rooms, and when they went out once a day to report to Captain Alexander, instead of remaining in the heart of the city they would take a quiet stroll along the James [River]. Of course Captain Alexander had recommended them to the landlord, and they were receiving all the attention necessary to make them comfortable, and in a physical sense they were, but in a moral sense they were not.

They could not go out of their room, whether to the parlor or to the office, without coming into contact with the Confederate officers, and this they did not relish for the reason that they were not in position to close the mouths of the loud-talking gentry. So one day they asked Captain Alexander if he did not know of some private family where they could find a home for the time being. He told them that one of his friends could no doubt accommodate them, that he would see him and let them know the same day.

The result of this was that on the same night they were elegantly installed at the house of Major Denson, who lived on Capitol Square.[5] The family of the major was small: himself, his wife, and two daughters of eighteen and eleven years respectively. The house was large, and the whole second floor, nicely furnished, became the temporary home of our friends; and as they wished to live alone as much as possible, arrangements were made to have their meals served in their own rooms. Among the furniture was a piano, which Aramis at once appropriated to his own use.

Now, here was a place where they were perfectly secluded, where they could enjoy perfect quiet, where they could talk without fear of detection; and as they always spoke French, there was little danger of this anyway. The view from their windows upon the square was delightful, and the beautiful trees in the park around the capitol added much charm to the location.

On Monday, the 21st of April, they were sent for by General Winder, who informed them that he had been unable to reach the man who had made charges against them, and that, moreover, as the Federals had occupied Fredericksburg, where General McDowell had established his headquarters, there was no chance left to proceed with the investigation. Besides, the relationship of one of them with General Polignac and the information received from the French consulate as to the status of their respective families, as well as their conduct since they were in Richmond, had led him to conclude that the charges against them could not be sustained.

Therefore he would release them from all further restraint so far as their movements were concerned. Their arms were also returned to them, and an indescribable sense of pleasure thrilled through them when they once again had those trusty friends in their possession.

"General," said Athos, "it is due to you that we should tell you that we started from Washington to see General Polignac; that we started on foot, and finding the roads fearfully bad, we decided upon securing horses. We went to the farmer in Prince William County, one John Walker, and asked to buy three horses; he told us that he had no horses to spare; we told him, 'we must have horses, and put your price upon those three.' He said he wanted two hundred dollars apiece; that price was extortionate, and was surely another means of refusal, so we concluded we would give him one hundred dollars in gold for each of the horses, and it was much more than they were worth.

"He gave them to us reluctantly, not because it was not money enough, but because he took us for Yankees. I presume he got mad at our manner of taking the horses, and hence his charges. One of the horses, my own, was killed by Colonel Lee's pickets, and the two others strayed off whilst we were being arrested.

"This is the truth, and the whole truth of the matter. We did not come here because we sympathized with the South; neither are we here as Federal emissaries; we owe allegiance to neither, and most cordially thank you for your kind treatment of us."

CHAPTER 10

Plan for the Kidnapping

AS SOON AS THEY REACHED THEIR ROOMS, D'ARTAGNAN AND ARAMIS had a regular set-to with their swords as a matter of exercise and for the fun of it. Both were experts; so much so, indeed, that they might have fenced the whole day away without leaving a chance for the other to send a successful thrust home; and Athos was even better than they were in the art of fencing.

"Now then," said D'Artagnan, "for business! Have you been thinking of some plan to bring about that which we have come here for?"

"No, indeed," said Aramis, "I have been thinking of nothing at all, for fear that I might think aloud and bring on an explosion. I have been obliged to exercise more patience than I ever did in my life, especially at the hotel where my hand often felt like striking some of that insolent and long-haired gentry of South Carolina."

"And you, Athos?"

"Why, I have long since been letting you do all my thinking, D'Artagnan, as you ought to know."

D'Artagnan, without saying anything to his friends, had been thinking over the subject ever since he had arrived in Richmond, and had long since come to the conclusion that it was an impossible task to kidnap Mr. Davis, until he read in the *Richmond Dispatch* one day about the president taking his usual trip to Norfolk on board his tug. Then the idea at once occurred to him: "We must get possession of [the tug.]"

"Well," said D'Artagnan, "by reading the papers every day, I have found out that President Davis occasionally goes down by boat to Norfolk; he goes down there on a steam tug. In our strolls along the river we have seen that tug, and I have thought that if we could manage to get aboard of her some day when Jeff Davis is on board, we might run her by Norfolk to Fortress Monroe."[1]

"Easy as good morning," said Aramis.

"You think so?"

"Well, the way you put it, dear D'Artagnan, it seems very simple."

"Yes, but there are always a dozen men or so on board. However, I think this tug business is the *modus operandi* that will prove the easiest, and I am going to study the question at once."

"But will the authorities at Norfolk allow the tug to run by?"

"Why not? They know her, and that she belongs to Jeff Davis," said D'Artagnan. "She will fly the Confederate flag as usual, and they will simply imagine that Jeff Davis wants to find out something or other,—as he certainly will if we are on board. Once past Norfolk, we are out of reach.

"At any rate, as I said, I am going to study the possibilities of this scheme. I mean to find out what the tug generally does on the way to Norfolk, and when she arrives there; whether she would be likely to be fired upon if she did not stop. Now is the time when we are going to miss Porthos more than ever; his strength would be of such great assistance."

"How far is it to Norfolk?" asked Athos.

"Some hundred and ten miles. The tug runs down in eight hours and comes back in twelve, and I mean to take a trip down with her if I can, so as to be posted on the formalities used on the way."

"Take a trip down there? Can we go as passengers, paying our way?"

"Oh yes, but on some other steamers, not on the tug. But it is upon the tug with Jefferson Davis on board that we must undertake the trip. If I can find out that this is possible, I assure you that he will not come back here until Abraham Lincoln has had an opportunity to offer him his hospitality.

"Twelve men on board; and only three of us! The question becomes one of arithmetic, that is all, and should read, 'How are three men to dispose of twelve?' When I have found the proper method of elimination,— and I expect you to help me,—our task for the remainder will become easy. Mr. Davis will go on board of his own free will and accord, as he has done frequently, and will not come back inasmuch as we must and will find the means to obtain control of his conveyance on the way. Just think how much easier the work becomes since Mr. Davis goes on board of his own consent!"

"Famous scheme!" said Athos. "And as Aramis said a little while ago, 'easy as good morning' under favorable circumstances; and money, of which we have plenty and can get more if necessary, can take care of the circumstances. Then too, if anything were to go wrong on the way, I am enough of an engineer to blow up the tug, Jeff Davis and all, at a moment's notice."

"This is the ugly side of the affair and ceases to be arithmetic. Athos, pray let D'Artagnan make the calculations. I decidedly object to blowing-up part of the program."

"Oh, have no fears," said D'Artagnan, "when I give the word 'Ready!' everything will be so arranged that there will be no hitch in the proceedings. By the way, I have found out that there are eight belonging to the crew of the tug, besides Mr. Davis and his friends, which in round numbers make a total of twelve, not more, perhaps less. Three of the crew are negroes and they do not count."[2]

"That is right," remarked Aramis. "That is elimination and belongs to arithmetic; remainder, nine!"

"All right; oh, if Porthos were only here, and how sorry he is going to be! Athos, do you remember Roanoke [Island]? Aramis, we had a solid little brush with the Rebels there, and do you know what Porthos did?"

"No, please tell."

"Well, he took two Rebels by the throat, one in each hand, and lifted them bodily from the ground, guns and all, and knocked the backs of their heads together until their skulls cracked. Ever since he has been known as Porthos."

"Bravo, Porthos! How I wish he could get hold of Mr. Davis and General Smith in the same way!"

"His strength is simply prodigious. In a hand-to-hand fight he seldom used his weapons, but his fists make a regular rain of sledgehammer blows, which terrorizes much more than weapons do, and are much more effective, for every man he touches when he is at it, is either a dead man or altogether unfit for further use. No wonder D'Artagnan misses him in his elimination calculations."

Jefferson Davis had been pointed out to them once by Captain Alexander when the latter was on a visit to them. He was at the window when Davis happened to go by with a little girl, his daughter. Davis had just come out of the War Department, located at one of the corners of the square, and every day almost he went there at about the same time in the afternoon, and nearly always with his daughter he passed under the windows of the men who were conspiring against him. His residence was near Capitol Square.

One day Aramis wished to try the effect of his voice upon Davis, and sang the *Marseillaise* in the French while the president walked by under the windows. The latter was so charmed with the voice that he stopped to listen while Aramis, accompanying himself upon the piano, went on with the soul-stirring song, and Davis stopped until Aramis finished it. Several other people who happened to go by had also stopped, and he as well as they clapped their hands in recognition.[3]

The following day Aramis sang one of his most beautiful and difficult selections when the president was passing on his way home, and again he stopped to listen. Mr. Davis had seen much of the world; he had heard the very best of singers and was a judge. He came to the conclusion that the singer was an artist of the very highest merit; but who could he be? He inquired from one of the bystanders whose house this was. He was told that Major Denson lived there. "Ah, I know him well; I will ask him."

Major Denson was connected with the Ordnance Department of the Confederate States and was every day at the War Department, where he frequently met the president.

CHAPTER 11

Mr. Mercier in Richmond

IT WAS ABOUT THIS TIME THAT MERCIER, THE FRENCH MINISTER AT Washington, went to Richmond on business for his government. The Rothschild [banking house of Europe] had bought a large lot of tobacco in Richmond just previous to the war for the French government, which, owing to the sudden beginnings of hostilities and the blockading of the Southern ports, could not be shipped to France. Minister Mercier had been granted leave by U.S. Secretary [of State William Henry] Seward to take the necessary steps to secure this tobacco, and it thus became necessary for him to go to Richmond where the tobacco was stored. In Richmond his business was strictly with Mr. [Judah] Benjamin, then acting Secretary of State; he did not seek to see, nor did he see, Mr. Davis at all.[1]

As soon as our friends heard that Minister Mercier was in Richmond they at once called upon him, and great was his surprise to see them, as may well be imagined. They told him that they were on their way to see General Polignac when they had been arrested and came well-nigh being tried as horse thieves and spies.

"Well," said he, smiling, "this is very rich; but then you ought to know that in times like these one cannot cross the lines with impunity."

"Yes," said D'Artagnan, "we have found it out and I am wondering how we will manage to get out of here."

"Well, perhaps you had better go back with me."

"You are very kind, but we have not yet seen Polignac; we have just been released."

"Very well, remain then, and give my regards to the prince when you see him. Mr. Benjamin will dine with me today and I will speak to him of you, or have you met him already?"

"No, we have not," was the answer. "I think it would help us very much if you would tell him that we are not vagabonds."

"If you manage to come here at about seven o'clock, we will be through with dinner and I will introduce you. I would invite you to dine with me if you had met him. But as you have not, it is due to his position that I should have his consent."

"Have you succeeded in securing the tobacco for France?" asked Aramis.

"How do you know I came for that?"

"We saw it in the papers this morning."

"Well, yes, I have succeeded; in fact, I had succeeded before I came, and it took me about four months to arrange matters. I came, under flag of truce to Norfolk, and there chartered a steamer for this place. I will leave as soon as the tobacco is on board, probably during the afternoon tomorrow."

"Before you leave, Minister Mercier," said Aramis, "be so kind as to tell the French consul to let us have all the money we may require."

"Make a note of that," said the minister to a clerk who had come from Washington with him and who was writing at a desk in the room.

"I hope," said Aramis, "that my cousin, the secretary of the legation, is well?"

"He is, indeed, and would surely have wanted to come with me had he known that you were here."

They took their leave soon after, and in the evening at the specified time they sent up their cards and were at once introduced. The minister treated them almost as if they had been his own sons, and told Mr. Benjamin: "Mr. Secretary, these are the young men I have spoken to you about a short while since. Inasmuch as you were kind enough to grant my request for their introduction to you, I have now the pleasure to present them," and he enumerated their names and qualities.

Mr. Benjamin was a splendid-looking gentleman of about fifty years of age, with remarkably black hair and eyes; he was not tall, but heavyset; he was most affable and very sympathetic. He spoke French like a Frenchman, and of course the whole of the conversation between him and the minister was in French, as the latter never spoke English unless strictly obliged to do so.

"Gentlemen," said Benjamin, "this introduction by His Excellency opens to you the doors of my home at any time it may please you to call, and I will be most happy to serve you."

"By the way, Mr. Secretary, this young man," said Mercier, pointing to Aramis, "is a cousin of General Polignac, whom he and his friends are on their way to visit. He bears one of the proudest names in Europe, is heir to the richest estate in France, besides being very wealthy in his own name. But he has even better than all this; he has a voice without an equal and is the best singer of France and Italy."

"Oh, oh! He must be the gentleman whom President Davis heard. Where do you live, sir?"

"At Major Denson's, Capitol Square."

"Precisely! The president told me that passing by there on his way home, he accidentally heard you a couple of times and could not proceed on his way home until you had finished."

"Indeed," said Aramis, "I had not the least idea that the president was stopping on the street to hear me. I assure you, Mr. Secretary, that had I known of it, he would have been invited in. I will close the windows hereafter, or better still, I will have the piano moved to a back room."

"I would be much obliged to you, if one of these evenings you and your friends would give me the pleasure of your company at my residence. The president will then be able to enjoy your singing; he is exceedingly fond of music."

"I hold myself at your service, Mr. Secretary, and will deem an invitation from you an honor as well as a pleasure."

"I need not tell you, Mr. Secretary," said the minister, "that any kindness you may show these young men whom I hold in great affection will be deemed a kindness to me."

Mr. Mercier invited them to take breakfast at eleven next morning with him, and they left. He told Benjamin after their departure that the two others were also of excellent families, independently rich, and that they had been officers in the French army, that they had resigned their commissions to take service in the Federal army just for the fun of the thing, and that their regiment had been mustered out in March last, thus leaving them quite free of their movements.

When D'Artagnan and his friends had reached their rooms, D'Artagnan said: "I do not like this invitation. It is likely to lead to many others, and we have no time to spare; but then it could not be avoided, and was none of our seeking. Does it not look bad to you, my friends, to accept the hospitality and kindness of people against whom we conspire?"

"It does," answered Athos, "but then as you say, it is not our fault, and who knows; it may be all for the best after all. We do not mean to take advantage of their kindness; we do not mean to sell any secret we may find out, and their anxiety to hear Aramis sing cannot be allowed to interfere with our plans."

"I do not think," said Aramis, "that we should have any scruples at all in the matter, and so long as we do not use their kindness to their own personal detriment, our consciences are safe. I assure you that if I could I would play the part of a Siren with my singing, to lull Davis and his men aboard the tug in blissful forgetfulness. I would not hesitate for a moment to play the part that Jason is said to have played on board his ship *Argo*. Instead of Jason, it would be Aramis; in place of the *Argo*, it would be the tug; instead of the Fleece, it would be Jefferson Davis; and there would be no fable about it."

"Well," remarked D'Artagnan, "it is, after all, only making friends in the enemy's garrison, and there can be nothing dishonorable about it so long as the means are honorable. We are playing a big stake, single-handed so to speak, against millions and our cunning has to take the place of armies. Of course I do not refer to the risks we are running, inasmuch as we knew of them when we undertook this job. Our lives are as nothing.

"I do not believe that the war will be ended in case we succeed in taking Mr. Davis; this war has to be fought out to a finish. But then the kidnapping of Jefferson Davis from his capital by only three men will cover the Southern cause with mountains of ridicule, and the latter is a weapon that hurts of ten times even more than powder or sword. The question of what will be done with Davis should we succeed is for President Lincoln to decide."

"By the way," said Aramis, "have you seen Miss Alice Denson, the daughter of our landlord? She is one of the prettiest girls I ever saw!"

"Have a care, Aramis; it is forbidden fruit," laughed Athos.

"To be sure; I say it in all honor. I have never spoken a word to her, and do not expect to do so. When I accidentally meet her I hardly dare look at her."

"Too funny!" laughed D'Artagnan. "Here is a man that would not hesitate at jumping in the very jaws of death, yet is afraid to look at a pretty girl of eighteen."

"Yes, and explain it who may. I cannot. I never knew myself to be such a dunce with a girl before, and I will come to hate her, I presume, if the spell continues."

"Or, who knows?" said Athos. "Perhaps love her!"

"Don't say such things, Athos, or I'll go back to Washington with Minister Mercier tomorrow."

CHAPTER 12

The Flowers

POOR ARAMIS! HE KNEW NOT HOW TRULY ATHOS HAD SPOKEN. CUPID'S quiver was even then doing its silent work upon as noble and manly a soul as ever women held captive.

He had never spoken a word to Miss Alice; indeed, he had only seen her a very few times, and then by accident, either on the steps or in the hall as he went in or out of the house. As he had stated to Athos, he hardly dared look at her. Like himself, the others had never spoken to her; like himself, out of politeness they had saluted, and like himself again, they had seen that she was beautiful. But unlike him, they did not feel justified, beautiful as she was, in saying as he had said: "One of the prettiest young ladies I ever saw!" And unlike him, again, they had dared to look at her, and she had dared to return their respectful salutation with the semblance of a smile.

Would she have done the same with Aramis? Ah, there is the question!

She did not know; the look of her eyes upon those of Athos and D'Artagnan was simply the same as that she gave other men; but when it came to the look of her eyes upon those of Aramis, the sensation was different. Why? Because he lowered his? Perhaps. Who can explain the mystic relation that establishes a path between two hearts, and forges a chain betwixt two souls? All three were strikingly handsome and young; but if anything, in appearance Aramis was more youthful,—the others, his seniors by two and three years, looking more manly, always an additional charm in the estimation of woman.

But then she knew that Aramis was the singer. She asked her father one day, and he had pointed toward him; and every time he sang, he very unwittingly worked his mastery more and more deeply into that virginal soul. His looks were as nothing, they were immaterial; it was the voice that had charmed her, that had spoken to her heart, and finding at the same time that he who sang so sweetly was also handsome, she had quietly surrendered even before the surrender had been implored.

Not the least idea had Aramis of this, and she would have died rather than reveal the secret he could not guess, which he did not seem to care about. "Oh, why does he not guess!" she had perhaps exclaimed within herself. And perhaps,—as he had stated to Athos when teased about her, "I will come to hate her,"—she had exclaimed: "Oh, I will come to hate him if he does not guess the secret of my heart!"

Aramis felt sad, and quietly seated himself at the piano. It was then ten o'clock, and everything in the house and upon the street was quiet. He expressed his grief by singing variations of "The Heart Bowed Down," variations composed by himself to suit his voice, in a manner that brought tears to the eyes to both D'Artagnan and Athos. Oh, what pathos he put into the words, and how pure and melodious the tones. Both of his friends were sitting by the window when he commenced, but they soon found their way to his side, each with a hand on his shoulder, and when he had finished said: "Now Athos, let this be a lesson to you. Every time you mention the subject, I will punish you in the same way."

"Dear Aramis," answered Athos, with his voice full of emotion, "such a punishment as you have inflicted upon us just now, we are willing to endure to our dying day. I wonder whether the angels in heaven can make music sweeter than you have just made."

"It will be time enough for you to find that out when you get there," and Aramis retired to his room, bidding his friends good night.

"Hurry, D'Artagnan, hurry, or we won't be able to get Aramis away from here."

"I am doing all I can, and I dare say that within two weeks I shall say 'Ready!'"

"God grant it, and may it not be too late, even then!"

The next morning at seven as usual, our three friends were taking their coffee and Aramis was himself again. D'Artagnan went out immediately and promised to be back in time to go to Minister Mercier's breakfast.

At nine the servant girl who usually attended them brought in a beautiful bouquet with a card upon which was written, "To him who sang 'The Heart Bowed Down.'" She handed it to Athos, who, after reading the card, told the girl to give it to Aramis. He read the card and immediately flew into a passion.

"Who sent this?"

"I do not know, sir; it was brought by a messenger."

"Give it back to him. I do not want it!"

"But he is gone, sir," and the poor mulatto girl was almost dead with fear at the young man's anger and remained speechless before him, unable to move.

"Away with them, away! I take no flowers unless the name of the sender is with them; take them away! Don't you hear?"

"But don't you see," said Athos, "that you scare that poor girl out of her wits, Aramis?"

"Here," and he gave her some money, "I don't want to scare you; I am not angry with you, my child, but do take those flowers away. They make me sick."

Athos quietly led her to the door and told her to throw the flowers away.

"Why, good God," said Athos, "you are more sensitive than a colt under the spur! Some admirer sends you flowers and you fly into a rage that scares that poor slave almost into fits."

"But why do they not send the name with the flowers?"

"Why? Well, do you not expect a lady to give herself away in such a manner do you?"

"It seems to me that if she is afraid to send her name, she fears some indiscretion on my part that might compromise her, and we are not that kind of people, are we?"

"To be sure, but how does she know what we are?"

"I guess I will have to quit singing, and I do love it so much. How I wish we could take Davis away today and leave this place forever; and yet, Athos, I feel so happy here. Can you explain?"

"Yes, my friend, I understand the situation perfectly. You are in need of some violent emotions; your heart has indulged in the sweetest of sentimentalities and you are not even aware of it. But have some patience; the great work of our lives will soon be ready. And have no fears as to receiving flowers again. Our girl would rather die than bring any others here, I verily believe. Promise me, dear Aramis, that whatever may happen, you will not allow anything, *anything*, do you hear, to stand between you and us, until we are once again in Washington?"

"I promise you, Athos," said he, giving him his hand, "I promise it to you upon the love I bear my mother and sister."

"Thank you, Aramis, thank you."

CHAPTER 13

Mr. Mercier Leaves

D'ARTAGNAN'S TASK WAS ONE THAT REQUIRED EXTREME CAUTION; THE very least indiscretion would not only have proved disastrous to their scheme, but fatal to him and his friends. Of the three, he was by all means the best calculated for the work.

Already he had made a speaking acquaintance with the engineer of the tug, who was a New Orleans Creole, and that morning he went to see him on board the tug. It was the first time he went on board the craft. There was nothing particular to be seen on board such a small vessel, but the Creole showed him the president's cabin, which occupied all the spare space. Even small as it was, ten by ten, it contained a table, a washstand, and a very few chairs, most of them rockers. Around the sides were benches which at night were used as bunks.

No arms of any kind could be seen on board. He discovered that the president usually came on board at about ten at night, and reached Norfolk at six in the morning, leaving the latter place in time to reach Richmond by nine in the evening. The tug carried coal enough to go and return, but took a fresh supply of water at Norfolk. It never stopped on the way, and the reason why Mr. Davis went to Norfolk was to watch the progress and hurry the repairs on the *Virginia*, so as to enable him to send her out as soon as possible.[1]

The change of base by General McClellan from Alexandria to Fortress Monroe was giving great concern to President Davis, and he thought the sooner he could send out his *Virginia* the better it would serve to delay the Federal advance on the Peninsula: hence his anxiety and efforts to hurrying on the work. Had Mr. Davis succeeded and his iron-clad been ready to put out to sea, it goes without saying that all the Federal shipping in Hampton Roads would have been driven away or destroyed, thus cutting off from Washington City General McClellan's new base of operations. This, however, was not to be the case.

Having seen all there was to be seen on board, and having found out some particulars of great importance without even asking for them, D'Artagnan in return for the Creole's kindness invited him to dine for the next day, expecting thus to further improve his acquaintance with the man who was to all intents and purposes the master of the president's tug. He got back to Capitol Square just in time to get ready to start with his friends to join the French minister at breakfast.

The minister received them with his usual kindness, and after breakfast, at about one o'clock, the minister started for his steamer accompanied by his friends. The tobacco was all aboard, and everything ready for immediate return to Norfolk.

"By the way," said Mercier, "you may look for an early invitation to a reception at Secretary Benjamin's. I hope you will cultivate his acquaintance; you will find him a most agreeable gentleman."

He was given letters by our friends for their parents to be mailed in Washington, also one for Porthos, and then [they] bade the minister their adieus. The steamer veered around with prow downstream, and was soon lost of sight.

Then they walked back, and on their way crossed a place known as the Esplanade, a vast piece of land used as a promenade and a place for children to play, but which had now become, so to speak, a military camp. It was surrounded with barracks for the soldiers, the space in the middle being a large parade and drill ground. But great was their surprise to see in the middle of this place a very high gibbet, fully twenty-five feet high, with a crosspiece on the top, at one side of which hung a human form shrouded in black.

Athos asked one of the men around who it was that had been hanged. He was told that it was a Federal spy that had been executed in the morning, and that he would remain hanging until sundown, when the corpse would be taken away and interred in the potter's field. This sight created quite a sensation upon our friends, as they had never seen such a thing before. Besides, strong and brave as they were, they realized that they were just then engaged in a work that might lead them to the same fate.

Soon afterwards they were in their rooms.

"Just think of it," said Aramis, "and that is the fate which the infernal scoundrel who accused us of being spies had in contemplation for us. If I ever get back to Washington I vow that I will make him another visit which he will never forget."

"Yes, the fellow evidently had no love for us," said Athos.

"Neither is there any lost," replied Aramis.

"We can thank our stars, my friends, for the good fortune that has attended us so far," said D'Artagnan, "although there is no likelihood that we could ever have been convicted as spies, no matter how much the rascal lied. But to be forewarned is to be forearmed; and as we are engaged in even a more dangerous business than the one of which we were accused, I will this very day secure some violent poison which in case we become victims of an accident will enable us to escape the hideous fate while alive at any rate. Once dead they can do what they please."

CHAPTER 14

The Heart Bowed Down

THE LANDING OF GENERAL MCCLELLAN'S FORCES AT FORTRESS MONROE had created quite a panic in Richmond, especially since the attack on Yorktown had commenced; and this very day our friends could see that the Confederate Congress, then in session in the capitol, opposite their rooms, was making preparations to move away. Army wagons were around the building, and boxes were being put upon them to be taken away to the depot to be sent towards Montgomery.

However, word was received that day from the Confederate forces in front of McClellan, which quieted the feeling, and the Congress decided to remain in Richmond. But steps were at once taken to fortify the Rebel capital. Until this time not a fort, nor a ditch, had been made; true, Richmond is naturally well defended by the James and the Chickahominy, but strong as its natural position is, it could not have been defended for twenty-four hours against a victorious army that had just swept the Peninsula.

From that day on, work on fortifications was pushed most vigorously, and it soon resulted in as complete a system for defense as any place that the Confederacy possessed, Vicksburg not excepted. However, it was all labor lost. Those fortifications proved of no avail in the end, since Richmond eventually fell without even an attack upon them.

Whether it would have been wiser for the Rebels not to have fortified Richmond at all, but to remove the government and archives as soon as it became indispensable to their safety to some point far remote from the contending armies,—and by this means have allowed the Army of

Virginia under the able generalship of Robert E. Lee, to do effective work elsewhere,—as is yet an open question, the discussion of which is, if not altogether foreign, at least superfluous to the purposes of this narrative. But it can nevertheless be stated as a proposition that cannot easily be controverted, that Richmond as a capital was an element of weakness to the South; it paralyzed, or at least confined, the services of the ablest general and the flower of the Confederate army within limits altogether too narrow for the scope of their possible usefulness; it made Antietam and Gettysburg possible, both of which were disasters which the South was never able to overcome.

"Well, D'Artagnan, what news?" asked Athos.

"I have been on board the tug,—at least so they call her, but she has ceased to be a tug for the present. I am making friends with the biggest man on board, namely the engineer, with whom I have had a speaking acquaintance for a few days already. Tomorrow he comes to dine with us, as I want him to take a liking to us all. He is a New Orleans Creole, of about thirty-five, and speaks French, I dare say much better than he does English. There are no arms on board the cutter; she goes from here to Norfolk without stopping, comes back the same way, leaving [Richmond] at ten at night to return the next night.

"I am not sufficiently acquainted with the engineer as yet to be able to judge of his character and do not intend to make him a confidant, anyway. The cook on board is an Italian, a most villainous-looking sort of an individual, fit to do anything, but never to be trusted. The negroes on board are, as I told you before, slaves; they belong to Mr. Davis himself. With the exception of getting on board at the opportune moment, I see my way clear to the successful termination of our scheme."

His friends had gathered around D'Artagnan, so that he spoke low enough for no one except themselves to hear what he was talking about. They followed him closely, and when he had finished the account, Aramis exclaimed: "At last!"

"But yet," remarked Athos, "the latter is a very important part, I should say."

"It is the most important, and it would block everything if our ingenuity did not find the means."

"Could we not hide ourselves on board until the time for operations arrive?" asked Aramis.

"No, the thing is too small to successfully hide anything; besides, hiding is subject to discovery, surprise, and alarm. It will not do. Judging from Mercier's conversation, we are soon to be invited to Secretary Benjamin's; the main object of this invitation will be to give Mr. Davis an opportunity to enjoy your singing, Aramis, and I want you that night to so work yourself into his good graces, as to be enabled to solicit of him soon after, the privilege for yourself and us, to accompany him on his trip, as a matter of curiosity to see the vessel he is in such a hurry to send out against the *Monitor* once more."

"Good enough; I shall have to seduce the old gentleman. And then?"

"And then? Well, the trick is played, that is all. There are only three men awake at once during the night: the engineer or his assistant, the fireman or his assistant, and the steersman or his assistant. We will bring these by some means or other under the influence of powerful narcotics, silence the others at our leisure. The slaves we intend to use for our own purposes, with promise of gold and liberty, after every white man is disposed of. We must each provide ourselves with a dagger; there must be no shooting done, and I hope there will be no necessity to shed blood; but if it becomes necessary, by the gods we must not hesitate."

"Hesitate!" exclaimed Athos. "The sight of that gibbet has sealed the doom of the poor wretches who would resist."

"We must find out from the Creole if the tug can go faster than she usually does; this is a great point," said D'Artagnan. "If we could gain an hour or so before reaching Norfolk and pass the place that much ahead of time, so much the better, for then Jefferson Davis would be called up at Newport News instead of at Norfolk. Go to sleep a soverign and awaken a captive! It will be hard. I would rather be shot, and perhaps so would he."

"D'Artagnan," said Aramis, "you discuss these things in a manner that makes me tremble."

"That is all right. Let us do all our trembling now, for there will be no time to do so after we are at it. We have a great deal to find out yet from the engineer, and I rely upon you, Athos, to post yourself about all such particulars as you may wish to know, for . . . you will have to take the throttle while Aramis and I are watching the rest."

"As a *coup de main*, I question if history will record its equal," said Athos.

Yes indeed, a feat like this would not only seem impossible but incredible, and yet its practicability, thanks to Mr. Davis's trips to Norfolk, made it comparatively an easy matter at the hands of three fearless men who were willing to sacrifice their lives, if necessary, in its execution.

The most admirable thing about it was not the daring,—so many daring deeds were being performed in those days,—but the devotion to the Federal cause shown by those three men, who were not even American-born, a devotion above and beyond all praise. It was not the act of mercenaries; they could not have been hired to do such work, and they would have scorned the very thought of financial reward. May their example serve as a lesson of the most exalted patriotism to the present and coming generations!

But what of those flowers that had been sent to Aramis in the morning? They had been sent by Miss Alice with the strictest injunction upon the servant and faithful slave to say they had come from the outside, and it has been seen how well she obeyed the instructions of her young mistress. When told to throw them away, she carried them back where she had received them, and then told Miss Alice all about the passion into which Aramis had flown and what he had said.

The servant was still trembling with fear, and her mistress herself took to trembling, and even to crying. But then she had sent him the flowers not as a token of love, at least she tried to convince herself; she had sent them as a complimentary appreciation of his singing the night before.

Oh, yes, that song had stirred her to the very utmost, and early in the morning she had secured the flowers, sent them as has been seen, and felt sad at their stormy reception. However, she became somewhat reconciled after she heard from the servant that the young gentleman had said he never received flowers unless he knew the name of the sender. He would have received them had she sent her name But then, how could she possibly have sent her name? To be sure, she had unbounded faith in his loyalty as a gentleman, but never would she have dared to send her card with the bouquet.

The poor girl pined all day long over the subject, finding plenty of excuses for herself in acting as she did, and yet at the same time not wishing to find fault with him. And so, deeper and deeper was Aramis unknowingly finding his way into her very soul. But how to let him know about those flowers? She quietly resolved to play that night upon her own piano the same tune he had sung the day before, the very same "Heart Bowed Down." He would undoubtedly hear it, and perhaps then he would guess the name of the incognita.

But, oh, how long those afternoon and evening hours were. Was ten o'clock ever to strike? She had time and again allowed her fingers to run over the keys of her instrument and, in a subdued tone, with the doors closed so as to be sure that no one upstairs could hear her, play the very same music he had played until she became satisfied that she could do it justice.

Ten o'clock, at last! Everything was quiet as the evening previous. Alice was alone below with the doors open; she tremblingly commenced to play. Gradually her touch of the keys became bolder and the pulsations of her heart stronger. Those who were still awake in the house could not fail to hear her, and our friends had not yet retired.

"Oh, oh," said Athos, "The Heart Bowed Down!"

"It is, indeed," said Aramis.

"Well, what of it?" asked D'Artagnan, who knew nothing of the flower scene of the morning.

"Oh, nothing," answered Athos, "except that Aramis received a blank card this morning, and that the name of the sender is probably being wafted upon the music from below."

"What shall I do, Athos?" asked Aramis in great perplexity.

"Do? Why, listen as we do; and when the player below has finished, let her know that you have heard her by answering in the same way. I think that will give you all the leeway necessary to speak to her the first time you meet."

Very soon the music ceased and the lid of the piano was heard to close. Aramis then quickly echoed the same music that had been played below. Alice heard it, and oh, how delighted she was just then; she knew he had heard her, and she knew that he now knew the name of her who had sent the flowers and that she was forgiven.

Aramis retired in a most happy frame of mind that night with visions of happiness crowding his slumbers, endeavoring to fight sleep away whenever on the point of falling asleep. Sleep seems a great disturber when one is happy. It means utter forgetfulness. Not to think when one can think of things so sweet to one's heart as Aramis had, he thought, the right to think of, was vandalism pure and simple. And yet nature finds the means to make us forget and to sleep more easily when happiness bids us to remain awake, than when misfortune cammands us to sleep. Nature can be ever so cruel, and that which was true for Aramis that night was also true for another heart under the same roof, and Alice wondered whether he would now dare look at her and speak as they met.

CHAPTER 15

A Visit to the Tug

D'ARTAGNAN ON THE NEXT DAY CONTINUED TO STUDY THE SEVERAL points in regard to the plan which he had determined upon, and expected to learn many particulars from the engineer while at dinner, which would enable him to clear up several points which as yet were somewhat vague in his mind. He told his friends about these, so that in the course of conversation between their guest and themselves, any point either overlooked or not made quite plain could be inquired into by the others. . . .

That same day in the afternoon they received the visit of the engineer. Things were made as pleasant for him as our friends could possibly make them, and it was a very late hour before they separated. All that could possibly be found out from him had been discovered, and the most important thing was that the negroes on board could if necessary steer the steamer to Norfolk as well as the engineer himself could, and that frequently one or the other of them was at the wheel.

Considering that our friends knew absolutely nothing as to the condition of the James River, this was indeed a most important discovery, as they had come to the conclusion that it was an absolute necessity for them to enlist the services of the three slaves; and they were correct in their surmise. Thus everything was ready for their enterprise, provided they could find their way on board, and Aramis was to make the first attempt for this through Mr. Davis himself if the opportunity presented itself; if not, D'Artagnan made bold to promise that he would find the means.

The next day D'Artagnan took his friends on board the tug so as to get them acquainted with the craft, and as she was very small this became an easy matter. They were received most cordially by the engineer, who showed them where he and his assistant slept, also where the cook and the other two white men had their berths. The negroes slept at the rear end of the tug between two decks, in a small place where it was impossible for a man to stand erect, a small hatch serving as window and door to their place of abode; and D'Artagnan at once came to the conclusion that this "rat hole" would be an excellent place to confine the crew after they had been securely gagged and pinioned, a thing which they intended to do after they had their prisoners under the influence of the narcotic which was to deprive them of their senses for the time being.

As to Mr. Davis they decided that he would be left in his own room, under the influence of a narcotic that would make him sleep a death-like sleep for a solid ten hours, all the time they thought necessary to go from Richmond to Newport News, or Fortress Monroe. They were not particular so far as the crew was concerned, even though force had to be used; but as to Mr. Davis they did not intend to touch a hair of his head. They were jealous to deliver him up in good condition and everything was to be made ready to that end.

Our friends had not the slightest doubt as to the success of their daring enterprise. So sure were they of it that they did not even think of their own lives which would have been forfeited had they failed. True, a man who undertakes such a desperate deed has no business to think of his own life, or he would never undertake it; besides, they had by now resolved in case of failure to blow up the tug, and Athos was firmly resolved to do so,—death from his own hands for himself and his friends being a hundred times preferable to ignominy. This was a point that had been discussed, had been agreed upon, and was irrevocable,—so much so indeed that the subject was never referred to again. . . .

Victor Vifquain, at age twenty-nine, wearing his Medal of Honor. COURTESY OF THE MASSACHUSETTS COMMANDERY, MILITARY ORDER OF THE LOYAL LEGION, U.S. ARMY MILITARY HISTORY INSTITUTE.

Civil War Richmond. COURTESY OF THE MASSACHUSETTS COMMANDERY, MILITARY ORDER OF THE LOYAL LEGION, U.S. ARMY MILITARY HISTORY INSTITUTE.

Camp Butler, Springfield, Illinois, where Vifquain joined the 97th Illinois after his mission to Richmond. COURTESY OF THE ILLINOIS STATE HISTORICAL LIBRARY.

The Battle of Fort Blakely, as depicted in *Harper's Weekly,* May 27, 1865. *Harper's* reported, "Probably the last charge of this war, it was as gallant as any on record."

The Vifquain family
(c. 1880). Clockwise
from left: John,
Victor Jr.,
General
Vifquain,
Elmer,
Blakely,
Caroline,
Gertrude,
Caroline
(daughter),
Charles,
Teresa.
COURTESY OF THE
VIFQUAIN FAMILY COLLECTION.

Victor Vifquain in Cuba
during the Spanish-
American War. COURTESY OF
THE NEBRASKA STATE HISTORICAL
SOCIETY.

Victor Vifquain (c. 1903).
COURTESY OF THE NEBRASKA STATE
HISTORICAL SOCIETY.

Victor Vifquain's final
resting place, Calvary
Cemetery, Lincoln,
Nebraska. COURTESY OF THE
VIFQUAIN FAMILY COLLECTION.

CHAPTER 16

Aramis and Alice

THE SAME DAY, AN INVITATION FROM SECRETARY BENJAMIN TO ATTEND A reception at his residence was brought by one of his secretaries, who delivered it in person to our young friends. He informed them, after having introduced himself, that Mr. Benjamin would deem it a great favor and would be very happy if they would accept the invitation, as President Davis was to be present, and he hoped that Aramis would do him and his guests the pleasure of indulging them with some of his musical selections. The visitor was informed that they expected to leave at an early date, but that if they were in the city they would deem it an honor to accept the invitation.

After the visitor had left, D'Artagnan remarked: "Now Aramis, here is your chance. We have no time to lose. I see in the papers that the Federals are advancing on the Peninsula, and Norfolk will either have to be evacuated by the Confederates at an early date or else the latter must repulse the Federals. We must go down to Norfolk as soon as possible."

"Very well, I will do my best to secure for ourselves an invitation from Mr. Davis to go down to Norfolk with him. But knowing as we do that we intend to betray his confidence and his hospitality in the most woeful manner, I feel some scruples that I must and will overcome."

"Yes, it is rather tough, but it has to be done. This is not a kindergarten picnic. We must set aside our finer sentiments and remember that we are just now adventurers bent on a mission that requires very great cunning if it is to be carried out successfully, and even then we may fail. I believe that we have selected the most merciful way to solve the problem, inasmuch as there is to be no bloodshed if everything goes as we most anxiously desire it to go. If bloodshed is resorted to, it will not be our fault."

This was the 6th of May. The invitation was for the 9th.

Athos, whose studies at the [Belgian Military School] had made him an expert chemist, charged himself with the duty of securing the most effective narcotics, and succeeded in doing so. He then showed D'Artagnan and Aramis how they had to be used, so that at the proper time there should be no failure in their application.

All three were full of glee over the seeming simplicity of the feat which they had at one time considered impossible. Mr. Davis, nor his friends, nor the world at large, ever knew how near he was to having been quietly removed from Richmond to Fortress Monroe and Washington in the month of May 1862. What an awakening it would have proven! The reason why he was not will soon be known.

Four or five days yet, days of the very greatest anxiety to be sure, and then our heroes would know whether or not they would be enabled to do that which they had resolved upon to accomplish. Meanwhile, to all outward appearances, they took time and things quietly, trusting to their good fortune for success.

Major Denson called upon our friends soon after Secretary Benjamin's invitation had been received, and begged them to meet his family in the evening. D'Artagnan was out, and Athos had as usual to do the honors, Aramis being struck almost speechless when the major made his errand known.

As soon as he had left, Athos remarked: "Have you heard, Aramis: do you feel equal to the task?"

"Yes, dear Athos. I will at last have an opportunity to speak to her. My heart beats harder and faster at the thought that it could possibly do had I to fight single-handed a whole regiment. Strange what spell that sweet girl has cast over me! I never had an idea that I could or would feel as I do."

"Aramis, my boy, that heart of yours has at last found its conqueror."

"But just think of it. I have never spoken to her; I could not, if I would, tell the color of her eyes. I have not seen her more than half a dozen times, and yet my soul seems to be hers."

"Precisely! It is the chapter of retribution. You have made so many girls giddy with the pretty things you told them, when in reality you did not mean one-hundredth part of what you said, not thinking that many a heart has ached and ached as the result of such flirtations. But now it is your turn, my good fellow, and I trust most sincerely that she will not prove as cruel as I have known you to be in Washington.

"Oh, Athos!"

"Aye, to be sure; I know well enough that you did not mean to be cruel. But what is going to be the result of all this?"

"I do not know."

It was indeed a serious question, and Athos was right when he asked. In the position in which our friends found themselves at the time, love was the very thing most to be avoided. True, Aramis was a man of honor; he knew that he owed himself for the time being to his two friends, whose very lives, as well as his own, would pay the penalty and become the forfeit of an imprudence on his part. Hence, there was no danger that Aramis would forget himself. Athos felt perfectly confident of that.

But the love of Aramis for the young lady,—and it is safe to say that his love was treasured in the heart of the maiden,—might bring about delays in the execution of the plan that they had conceived, and delays meant failure, as General McClellan was advancing on the Peninsula. However, there were only a very few days to wait before the drama was to take place on board the president's tug, and Athos intended to keep Aramis so busy during the time that it would prove difficult for him to become too seriously entangled in the meshes which Cupid was preparing for him.

"Tell me," said D'Artagnan as he stepped in, "do you remember what sort of a looking man he was?"

"Who?" asked Athos.

"Why, the Virginia farmer, John Walker by name, who gave us all the trouble. . . . It seems to me that I have seen someone who reminds me of him. If I remember rightly he had no beard, with the exception of a goatee of considerable length; the cheeks and lips were clean-shaven."

"Yes, that is he."

"Well, the person I now refer to has no goatee. He is growing young sidewhiskers and a mustache; he is lank, long and lean, and reminds me of our Virginian."

"We must make sure of this," said Athos, "and must hear him talk."

"How will you manage that?"

"By going right up to him and asking him if his name is not John Walker. He will answer, and then we'll know."

"Why, that's so; strange I did not think of it when I met the individual who aroused my suspicion. Athos, I believe I have lost half my wits since I put all my thought on the tug; but we have to make sure of this since he now owes us a revenge."

"Just put me in contact with the fellow," said Aramis, "and the question will soon be elucidated."

"But no! Coming to think of it, it will not do to have any trouble on our hands just now,—we would be sure to have trouble if we recognized his voice and took him to task for his accusation," said D'Artagnan. "All that is wanted is to make sure who he is, and then watch him. We might even tell Captain Alexander about it; he could ascertain if the fellow means us mischief."

"Yes," said Athos, "that will be the safer method. The captain knows that Walker falsely accused us, and that he may try it again since he was frustrated in his first attempt."

At six o'clock our friends sent their cards to Major Denson, and they were at once requested to enter. No one was present with the exception of the family and Captain Alexander, whose duty it became to introduce the young strangers to the ladies. Miss Alice looked supremely happy when Aramis bowed to her, and by her innate modesty and well-bred simplicity she made him feel at ease, and he found the means of interesting her from the start with his conversation, which required all her attention because of his French accent.

What he had dreaded so much,—how to approach her the first time,—had lost all of its terror, and yet, man of the world as he was, he had never felt in the presence of woman as he felt then. He wished to say things which he did not dare to say at their first meeting. She was conscious of this, and was thankful for his consideration of her feelings. What his tongue did not say, his eyes, however, expressed, and hers reciprocated. The language of the heart performed its duty. . . .

Just then a servant entered the room and handed a card to the major. After looking at it, he said: "Gentlemen, Major General Smith, lately arrived from Fredericksburg, an old acquaintance of ours, wishes to see us. Will you allow us to have him introduced?"

To which Athos replied: "Major, when we were detained as prisoners at Fredericksburg, the general did not treat us in a gentlemanly manner, and we prefer not to meet him, as we are not desirous to cultivate his acquaintance any further, especially in the presence of ladies. Therefore, we beg you to excuse us, and we thank you for the honor you have done us, and for the pleasure we have had in your company. I also wish to state that at an early date, say a week or so, we intend to set out for Mississippi."

There was nothing to reply, and our three friends bowed themselves out, greatly to the regret of all. They were followed by Captain Alexander, who said to the major, "I will soon return."

They passed by the general in the hall without paying the slightest attention to him,—the only manner in which they could insult him then and there. Captain Alexander bowed his recognition.

Our friends were very glad to see the captain come with them, as they always enjoyed his company. He was their first friend in Richmond, and, speaking the same language, there was also much natural sympathy between them. Then, too, he was a gay and jolly fellow, as well as a thorough soldier.

After being comfortably seated in the Frenchmen's rooms, enjoying the smoke of cigars, the conversation ran upon almost everything pleasant, and before taking leave the captain said: "I came with you not only to enjoy your company, but perhaps to render you a service, as well as to have a chat over the possible and immediate future, especially since you have announced your early departure. Of course you read the papers, but they do not always tell all that is going on; in confidence I will tell you that we expect great events to happen around here before long.

"General R. E. Lee, the best of our generals, has been ordered to the front to take command of all our forces, and he will leave at once. Of course we believe he will defeat General McClellan, for we have nearly as many men as he has, and the advantage of being at home with a perfect knowledge of the country.[1] But the goddess of war can be as fickle as any other goddess, and it is possible that the other thing may take place."

"What then?"

"Well, it is not as yet decided whether we shall abandon Richmond, and go to Montgomery, or maintain ourselves here. Possibly the latter. I dare say that as noncombatants and foreigners you do not wish to be around here if the worse came to the worst, and you may perhaps prefer to continue your journey to find General Polignac. To do that you will require passes from the provost marshal general, and I can secure these passes for you at once if you so desire."

"We were talking of the matter yesterday," said D'Artagnan, "and we did not know what steps to take. We are obliged to you for mentioning the subject and offering to help us out."

"It is the easiest thing in the world, when you have the proper passes, to travel from here to Mexico, but a practical impossibility if you have not. As you are not in a particular hurry, I would advise you to move horseback; our railroad system is none of the best, just now especially, and the army requires nearly all the lines; however, when you happen to strike a road that is not used for the transportation of troops, you can pay your way. The passes will take you anywhere in our lines, and you will at all times be under the protection of our military authorities."

"Well, we will accept your offer with infinite pleasure, and we shall thus be able to move when we are ready. Please remember that we have side arms and wish to take them along."

"As a matter of course. You may need them, too, as in some parts of the country, in the mountains for instance, the roads are often infested with deserters who have respect for nothing. Then, too, if Yorktown and Williamsburg fall, Norfolk will have to be evacuated, and our navy yard probably destroyed. It is said that President Davis, who is a great soldier as well as a great statesman, will accompany General Lee to the front to view the situation for his own satisfaction. Well, I must go; come tomorrow and take breakfast with me. I will have your passes ready."

And he descended to join the Denson family below.

CHAPTER 17

Confessions of Love

GENERAL SMITH AND CAPTAIN ALEXANDER HAD LEFT THE HOUSE together. Before parting for their respective homes, the general said to the captain: "Those young Frenchmen do not seem to have much regard for me. They surely recognized me, and should at least have bowed their recognition."

"It goes without saying that they recognized you, as I heard them say to Major Denson that they were not satisfied with the manner in which you treated them at Fredericksburg, when your card was received this afternoon. But not a word of censure was spoken by them against you, or of you, while I was with them."

"Do you know, Captain, that I still have some suspicion against them?"

"Have you? I have kept the very closest watch over them for nearly one month and I have seen nothing that makes me doubt that they are perfect gentlemen, and that the charges of horse stealing and spying were simply trumped up by the man who accused them."

"They told me all about the matter; they surely treated him with the upper hand, and he felt sore over it. They have been introduced to Secretary Benjamin by the French minister at Washington when he was here a few days ago, and the secretary takes sufficient interest in them to have invited all three to his reception for next Friday, the 9th."

"Well, perhaps I am mistaken. I will then be in the field, as I am ordered away, when the reception takes place, or else I would be there and have an explanation with them in regard to the slight they did me by passing near me as entire strangers. I know nothing against them with the exception of the charges made by the Virginia farmer."

"Charges which have been proved false," [said Alexander.] "I would rather take the word of any of those young men than that of a hundred such farmers as the Virginian, who does not see fit to join with us in fighting the Yanks while they are invading his very home. At any rate, these young men will soon leave to visit General Polignac in the southwest, from whence they will go to Vera Cruz , where no doubt they will find some steamer to take them back to their homes in France. Spies and horse thieves are not made of such gentlemen as they are. By the way, General, how about that suit of yours with Miss Alice?"

"I never saw much chance for me there, and really less than ever now. She treated me with considerable indifference this evening, to my very great surprise."

The captain was not surprised. He had seen Aramis and Alice together that afternoon and had detected, so he thought at least, the furtive glances of young people who have a secret between them.

"Well, here we part. Good luck to you, General, and good-bye."

The Frenchmen remained at home that evening, and all they had heard from Captain Alexander in regard to the evacuation of Norfolk and the possible destruction of the navy yard at that place discouraged them greatly. It was a sad evening for them, as it was evident that if Norfolk was evacuated the regular visits of Mr. Davis to the ironclad *Virginia* would cease, and his kidnapping thus become an absolute impossibility.

To be sure, they might remain at Richmond, but life would become exceedingly monotonous there without the incitement of the great deed they were contemplating. Their going to Mississippi was never seriously considered by them, and their proposed visit to General Polignac was more of a makeshift and make-believe than anything else.

They had no idea at all as to the probable result of the campaign then going on. If Richmond were evacuated within the next month or so, all well and good. This would have suited Aramis exceedingly well, but it might take months and perhaps years. . . . If their former plan was to be abandoned, there was only one thing left for them to do,—go where the fighting was going on rather than remain idle in the capital city.

They knew that the Rebels had about 100,000 men with excellent generals to lead them.[1] That army was made up of the flower of Southern yeomanry; it was the pride of the South ever since the battle of Bull Run had been fought and won by them. They were the bulwark over which the Federal army, with at least the same number of men under McClellan had to rush, and the result on the [6th] of May, 1862, was indeed problematical.

A great part of the evening was occupied in discussing several plans of action, but it was a difficult task to come to a satisfactory conclusion.

Nine o'clock had just struck when the colored girl made her appearance with a note in her hand. Remembering how Aramis had treated her once before, she hardly knew what to say or do.

"Well, my girl," said D'Artagnan, "do not be afraid. Tell us what you want."

"I would like to see Master Aramis."

He approached her and she handed him a note and retired. Aramis went to his room to read it, and then returned to his friends, who were considerate enough not to ask questions.

At ten o'clock they parted for their respective rooms, very much annoyed as to the poor prospects of their enterprise so far as Athos and D'Artagnan were concerned; not so Aramis, as the note he had received read: "Meet me in the parlor after all have retired tonight."

When Aramis received Alice's note he was struck with surprise. He did not once think about Athos's telling people below of their early departure in her presence, and that it might be the cause of her alarm. However, he was delighted at the thought that he would meet her and be able to confess his love, but would have been far happier had he known the real cause.

He had been several days in the house, and knew the time at which Major and Mrs. Denson usually retired; he also knew that Alice seldom remained any longer than they did. Her younger sister retired invariably at eight o'clock. . . . This evening, or rather night, Aramis had been on the alert, and he knew that the older people had retired when he ventured on the visit which was to determine his fate and that of Alice's love. In the parlor the lights were burning very brightly, and the door was wide open.

Alice, too, had been on the alert, and she met Aramis almost on the threshold, saying: "Is it really true that you are going to leave us?"

Her voice was full of emotion. She trembled; her eyes dimmed with tears. He took her hand and led her to a seat, as she could scarcely stand.

Then, with one knee on the floor, and looking into her sweet face, her eyes hardly daring to rise, he lifted her hand to his lips and kissed it. A faint smile appeared at once upon her face; her eyes finally fixed themselves upon his. Kissing her hand several times more in quick succession, he arose, keeping her hand clasped between his two, saying: "I was not mistaken, then; and I am not indifferent to you. Your heart has responded to mine since you wish me to remain."

She placed her other hand on his, and while bending her head over them he could feel her tears glide over his fingers, but she remained speechless.

"God is my witness," said he, "that if I could stay I would. Were I able to take you with me, I would, for I love you to adoration."

Rising to her full height, their hands still clasped, she looked him straight in the face with happiness beaming over her features and answered: "I need not tell you the secret of my heart,—you know it. My thoughts have been yours from the very first time I saw you; but now that you tell me of your love, oh, I am ever so happy. I am proud of your love. I am ready to follow you wherever your steps may be directed.

"Do not go away! If you do, take me with you; to part now that we can be so happy has terrors for me. It seems that our parting will be forever. To have you in the house, to know that you are here, even though knowing nothing of your love, was supreme happiness to me. With you gone, knowing that you do love me, will be terrible misery."

She had spoken so tenderly that it affected him visibly; her hands were still clasped in his.

"Reasons of the greatest importance compel us to leave,—indeed it is a matter of honor with me; dear girl, nothing else could make me part from you. Neither can I at this time take you with me. It is absolutely impossible. Pray have confidence in me!"

"Oh, I have! My life is yours; it is the separation that I so dread. So much fighting is going on everywhere,—so many are being killed!"

"Listen, dear Alice. It will be some days at least before we leave Richmond. I will see you every day if you allow me, as we are doing now. Can we?"

"I will send word by Nancy if we cannot."

"I will tell you what circumstances control my every action at present, and tell you other things about myself that you should know, and will leave you to judge."

"Yes, oh yes, you must give me courage."

"Sweet Alice, after this mutual confession of love, we are as one, are we not?"

"Forever!"

"Then let one kiss seal our love and consecrate it."

He pressed her to his breast and she responded to the pressure. The beats of their hearts were as one, their souls blended, and their lips met in the very sweetest and chaste embrace.

"Now please retire, dear Maurice."

She tore herself away from him and they parted. For the first time, perhaps, he obeyed the command of a woman under similar circumstances; for if all this was a new experience, the revelation of a mystery to Alice, it was not so to Aramis. His obedience was the best evidence of his real and sincere love. . . .

Nothing but the thought of his early departure disturbed her slumbers that night; his dreams were of future happiness in his native land, at his home, where she would be his before God and man.

CHAPTER 18

John Walker

THE MORNING PAPER WAS ANXIOUSLY LOOKED FOR TO FIND OUT HOW matters were at the front, and the first thing that appeared to the eye was:

YORKTOWNE EVACUATED
GENERAL MAGRUDER FALLS BACK ON
WILLIAMSBURG.[1]
FEDERALS MOVE TOWARD NORFOLK.
ETC., ETC., ETC.

All this in large type; it was as disappointing to the Confederates as it must have been to our three friends,—to the former because it meant retreat, to the latter because it meant the probable failure of a plot upon which they had worked so faithfully and upon which they had looked with the greatest hope.

Norfolk evacuated meant the destruction of all Rebel property, such as comprised the famous arsenal, and all shipping that might have been of use to the Federals, and chief among these was the famous *Virginia*.

They hastily finished their breakfast, and D'Artagnan, the man of quick perception and great resources, spoke up: "The chances are one hundred to one that Norfolk will be evacuated within the week, that the *Virginia* will be blown up, and that Mr. Davis has made his last trip down the river. Williamsburg will fall as Yorktown had fallen, and the contest will have to be fought out nearer Richmond. I have been thinking and thinking of some other scheme, but we had struck the only really practicable one,—at any rate I was willing to stake my life on its success. Have you, Athos, any other plan?"

"No."

"Nor you, Aramis?"

"None."

"Let us go to Captain Alexander and get our passes," said Athos. "Events are progressing so rapidly just now that there is no telling what another day may bring forth. A panic and a stampede may take place among the people here, and impede us in our movements. What say you?"

"Come on, "said D'Artagnan, "we should do well to secure good horses this very day so that we may mount them at a moment's notice."

All this was not exactly what Aramis wished things to be; however, there was nothing for him to do but acquiesce to his friends' desires. His heart told him to remain close to the girl he loved, but as he had told her the night before, honor commanded him to go with his friends. Always lighthearted and gay, Aramis was more or less downcast, as he was well aware that he could not stay in Richmond; he had sworn to stay with his friends, and would have done so even without an oath. It never once entered his mind that he could allow his friends to work their way back within the Federal lines without him. They had faced all kinds of dangers together during the last month, and there was no telling what there was yet in store for them.

If his friends knew anything about his visit with Alice the previous evening, which is probable, they had sufficient regard for him to refrain from mentioning it. They had not fully decided what they would do, but to return within the Federal lines so as to take part in the battles that were sure to be fought in the vicinity was likely their most cherished desire. The more they saw of the Confederate troops, and they saw them all day long, the more they disliked them, especially the officers who seemed to them the most impertinent set of youngsters they had ever seen. Their very looks were significant of dash and bravery, but their haughty demeanor and the long Indian-like hair they had made them look ridiculous to our friends, who had never before seen such specimens of army officers.

The Frenchmen soon arrived in the narrow and hilly street where the office of the provost marshal for the city of Richmond was located. After waiting a short while they succeeded in reaching the captain.

"You see I am very busy," said Captain Alexander, "and it will take some time to finish the passes, as they have to be signed by General

Winder, the provost marshal general. But I will send them to him by a special messenger, and in an hour or so they will be back here. Go upstairs to the room where you have been once before as my guests. Make yourselves at home there; find some good cigars on the table, and I will join you for breakfast very soon."

And the friends proceeded to the room where for a while they had been confined as spies and horse thieves, and in great danger of the most terrible punishment. It was only a short time ago, and they had almost forgotten it. Such is youth. There, too, they had witnessed the sale of slaves which had so revolted Aramis that he almost created an alarm by singing "My Maryland." This room was now used as a sitting room fairly well furnished. They took chairs, lit cigars, and proceeded to make themselves comfortable. Presently the servants entered and prepared the table for breakfast.

"Well," said Captain Alexander as he joined his visitors, "here are the passes, and we will proceed to fill out the blanks, as I simply asked for three blank passes, signed and sealed."

"Is there much to be filled out?"

"No, simply insert your name, and add after the words, 'Allowed to Travel' the words 'With Side-Arms,' and sign your names in the left corner at the bottom. The signature of General Winder, by order of the secretary of war, with his seal, passes and protects you all over the South, and countersigned by me with my seal, it enables you to go and come just as you please. Your own signatures are for the purpose of identification."

"Very well, let us complete the work right now."

It was soon finished, and each put his own pass in his pocket. To them each pass was worth a fortune; more, liberty; still more, life; as it meant freedom to go and come as they pleased within the Confederate lines. They thought it would be an easy matter, when in the mountainous regions of Virginia, to elude the Rebel picket and enter the Federal lines.

"Well, gentlemen, let us sit down, and as it may be the last time we are together, let us breakfast well."

"Do not talk that way, Captain," said D'Artagnan, as they seated themselves. "We are all very young, and this war is not going to last forever. But it seems to me that the sound of those guns is somewhat nearer than three or four days ago."

"Yes, the Yanks are moving up, but they are still a long way off. The shooting you hear must be from some heavy guns fired from the Federal gunboats at Williamsburg, which we suspected will have to be evacuated."

"Captain," said Aramis, "make me a promise. When this war is over, come to Paris; find me there, and you will never regret having come to France," and as he sat next to Captain Alexander they shook hands over it, and thus made it a promise not to be broken.

They remained together quite a while and had a splendid time. As D'Artagnan mentioned the necessity of purchasing horses the captain said: "I will go with you and take you to the best stable of the city."

On the way there D'Artagnan detected the fellow whom he thought was the Virginia farmer; he was lounging at the very door of the stable where they went.

"Say, Captain, will you do me the favor to talk with that man? I think I know him, and want to hear his voice. Do it so as not to arouse his suspicions; I will be near enough to recognize the voice."

The captain, who was in undress uniform, did so without causing the slightest suspicion, and D'Artagnan heard the voice plain enough to recognize it as that of John Walker, but to all appearances did not pay the slightest attention. Then back in their rooms the conversation turned on their future movements.

"Well," said D'Artagnan, "I know all about it now. I heard the voice of the man I mentioned to you the other day, and it is that of the rascal who came near sacrificing us."

"How do you know?"

D'Artagnan told them what he had done while they were being shown the horses by the proprietor of the stable. "And now that I know who he is, I can keep my eyes on him; he has lost his terrors. You have your passes, have you?"

"Why, to be sure."

"Those passes are real God-sends to us; they relieve us of all the formalities to be gone through at the depots, or before leaving the city. They enable us to go where we please, when we please, how we please, and come back the same way."

"As to me," said Athos, "when I leave this place, I mean it to be for good. We can do nothing more here to help our cause, and we must find our way back to the Federal lines as soon as possible. While all this fighting is going on I would die of consumption if I had to stay here until McClellan takes this place."

"That's all right; I agree with you. But which way shall we turn to cross the lines? I hardly think we can attempt it direct,—we shall have to move westward and reach some place where the movement of troops is not so active. We must get out of this immediate sphere of action. What say you, Aramis?"

"Oh, I will as usual do just exactly what you please. Just give me one day's notice, and after that the sooner we get into the fray the better I will like it. And for God's sake manage it, if you can, to lead the way by the home of John Walker, who had us arrested as horse thieves and spies. I wish to get at him once, only once."

D'Artagnan and Athos knew how much it would cost Aramis to leave Richmond; they understood what he meant when he said: "The sooner we get into the fray the better," and they would have told him to remain in the city and allow them to go. But they knew him too well to make him such a proposition, which he would have deemed a mortal offense. They came together; their fate had been as one since they left Washington; they must remain as one until back there unless parted by death. That is the way Athos and D'Artagnan felt, and they were so positive that Aramis felt the same way that they did not even think about separating.

"Before leaving we must secure plenty of money, for there is no telling what may happen; and also a letter of credit from our consul here to any French agent in the South would not prove amiss. There is no telling where we may be driven. I think you had better attend to that in person, Aramis," said D'Artagnan. He assented by saying that he would attend to it the very first thing in the morning.

It was getting late, but none of them felt like retiring. The conversation was not so cheerful as it generally was; their spirits were not just then the buoyant ones we are acquainted with,—and all that because of the probable failure to carry out the plan they had so carefully concocted for the kidnapping of President Davis.

"Can't you devise any other plan?"

"No, Aramis; it was the only thing we had a possible chance of accomplishing. We cannot murder the man, and the only thing that I can see for us to do is to leave Richmond and recross the lines. I think we have done wonders although not accomplishing what we came for. Our failure is simply due to circumstances over which we had no control. Besides, there is no telling what we may have yet to do before we get back to Washington. This land has become a vast military camp, and if it were not for the passes we secured we would be in a real bad fix, and might be obliged to travel hundreds of miles to reach Polignac, and then find ourselves in still deeper trouble."

"The shortest route across our lines will suit us the best of all."

"I shall study the situation, and dare say that before forty-eight hours we may be on the road; so Aramis, take notice."

The next morning Aramis and Athos walked down together to the French consulate, and after sending in their cards were at once taken to the parlor where they were greeted by the consul, whom they had not seen since the French minister had left. He informed them that he had intended to call, but had been unable to leave his rooms; he had not deemed it prudent to correspond, but that he had a message to deliver to them which he had received two or three days ago from Washington. He drew an official letter from his pocket.

"There is a letter from Mr. de Beaumont, secretary of the French legation at Washington, your cousin. He tells me, as you see, to allow you to read those two lines."

Aramis read, "Porthos is nearly well; ready to start if necessary." Having read them he said: "Please answer in the same way, 'Tell Porthos not to come.' Will this go at an early date?"

"Our mail to and from Washington is not as regular as we would like to have it, but no matter how things turn out on the Peninsula I think my next letter will reach Washington within one week."

"Mr. Consul, we need some cash, say one thousand dollars in gold, and also a letter of credit to any of your colleagues in the South for such amounts as I may require. We intend to leave soon, and there is no telling where we may turn up."

The consul arranged the matter, and Aramis made drafts on Paris for the amount. Then bidding the consul farewell, away they went. Once in the street they spoke of Porthos.

"Good Porthos! Do you know he would come at once, and God only knows how, if we had sent him word to come."

"Yes, but if none of us were here just now it would be much better. Three is bad enough, four would be still worse under the circumstances. My dear Aramis, we are, in my opinion, to undertake the most dangerous part of our trip."

"That will suit me exactly, for I am sure I will be in a fearful humor after I leave this town. I do not intend to fight every Rebel at night, but neither do I intend to allow any one of them to look askance at me. Our swords and pistols will need to be looked after carefully before we leave."

"Why, my good boy, our swords and pistols have been ready for business all the time, for we never knew what another minute might bring forth, and they are ready now. Indeed, you must have been absorbed in the very sweetest of dreams not to have thought of this before."

"Yes, it seems to me that I have just gone through the happiest days of my life; it seems like a dream, but all too short. My only aim and only hope shall be to return here as soon as possible, as soon as the place is taken and we have become the masters. Then with Alice's consent, away to France!"

These two overconfident young men had no idea that it would take three years longer, even though [Federal] guns were a few weeks later battering the gates of Richmond at Mechanicsville only six or seven miles away.

On their return to the rooms, D'Artagnan told Aramis to telegraph Polignac that they would soon leave the city on their way to Mississippi.

"But why? We are not going there, are we?"

"I guess not, although there is no telling; it may, however, serve us in the future in case we get into trouble."

"All right, I see the point. I will ask Captain Alexander where the prince is, and also for a permit for wiring to him."

"Well," said Athos, "let's go to the stable, get our horses, and give them a trial. Let us go together."

That was agreed upon, and they at once went to the stable. The proprietor had been instructed to secure bridles, halters, and everything pertaining to the McClellan saddle equipments, as if for campaign purposes.[2] He had secured all these, and was paid handsomely for his trouble.

The horses were brought out, and after careful inspection to see that all they needed was in its place, the young men had the proprietor remove the holsters, and mounting their steeds, rode away, only stopping a moment at Captain Alexander's to secure the information that Aramis required about the telegram to the prince. The message was written there and then, and the Captain promised to send it immediately.

"Captain, we are going to take a ride and give our horses a trial."

"Have you your passes about you?"

"We have."

"Well, follow this road, go through the gates where your passes will be looked at. Follow the turnpike, and you can have a splendid ride. I would go with you if not so busy."

Away they went, giving a good trial to the horses, which they found to be really first-class animals. It was quite late when they returned.

At their rooms they found a note from the secretary of state, informing them that, owing to public matters, the reception to be attended by
President Davis was postponed, and begging them to accept his apologies.

"Things are getting worse, then," said Athos, "as tomorrow is the 9th
of May, the day of the reception. A sense of propriety will not allow
rejoicings while defeat is in the air."

CHAPTER 19

The Great Naval Battle

No APOLOGY IS NECESSARY FOR NOW DEVOTING A CHAPTER TO THE *Virginia*, since it was only some sixty days ago that she had made herself famous in the annals of the world's naval warfare; when, too, she was to have been the indirect means by which the kidnapping of Mr. Davis was to be made a possibility.

The battle at Hampton Roads had been fought [between the *Virginia* and the Union ship the *Monitor* in March 1862]; American genius had devised two vessels of unprecedented construction, one at the North and one at the South, which revolutionized all the navies of the world. They created an epoch, and a battle had been fought that once again, as once before, proved the mettle of which the American sailors are made, inasmuch as the sailors of the South as well as those of the North, were American sailors, commanded by American officers, reared at Annapolis.[1]

The design on the flags of each were somewhat different, but the colors were the same, as both sides fought under the red, white, and blue. Of the same blood, the same race, the same kin, the historian will never be ashamed to say of the people of the North, "They were Americans," or of the people of the South, they were their brethren. A legacy as old as the nation, slavery, had brought them face-to-face, imperiling the safety of a country much dearer to the North than the abolition of slavery, which to the South was deemed a crime against their birthright.

Then, too, the present generation is told but little of the great naval battle of the 8th and 9th of March 1862. Even the generation of that day is not aware of what went on there, and it may prove, if not a very pleasant, at least an instructive reminiscence of the dark days of the Republic.

At an early day floating batteries were recognized as indispensable by the Confederate government, in order to defend their coast; however, they were short the means of building hulls or making engines. As luck would have it, the government of the United States had, in 1855, decided to build three powerful steam frigates, each of nearly 4,000 tons burden, and one of these, the *Merrimack*, happened to be at Norfolk, Virginia, for repairs in March 1861. As it was impossible to take her to northern parts [when Norfolk was captured by the Confederates], she was scuttled, set on fire, and sunk. She carried forty guns of heavy caliber.

The Confederate authorities, being in immediate need of a floating battery, took steps to raise this vessel after it had been examined and found that the lower part of it and the greater part of the machinery was not much injured. The *Merrimack* was raised, and an armored casemate of an entirely new model was constructed on her gun deck, thus making her the most powerful fighting machine that had ever been afloat.

She proved herself impervious to any kind of shot manufactured at that time, and broadsides at point-blank range had no effect upon her. The walls of the casemate being at an angle of forty-five degrees, the projectiles glanced off her deck and reached far beyond to be lost in the deep sea.[2]

The sight of this ship, renamed the *Virginia*, must have been extremely provoking and discouraging to [the Federals], when, on March the 8th and 9th, they were set upon by this monster of the seas in Hampton Roads. But the gallantry of the men was indescribable, for under the circumstances they knew that they were doomed to destruction, inasmuch as the boarding of the *Virginia* by [Federal] sailors was a human impossibility owing to a steam-scalding apparatus that had been contrived all around her deck.

The armament of [the *Virginia*] consisted of eight 11-inch guns with a 100-pound rifled Armstrong gun at each end. She was also provided with a powerful ram. Her draught of water was twenty-five feet, and her speed about eight knots.

[Federal] naval authorities were aware of what was going on at Norfolk, and they took steps to meet the old *Merrimack*, now the *Virginia*. Large sums of money were appropriated, and out of all this came the far-famed *Monitor* of [naval engineer] John Ericsson, who so named it, as he himself said, "in order to admonish the South of the fate of the rebellion, Great Britain of her fading naval supremacy, and the English government

of the folly of spending millions in fortifications for defence." Mr. Ericsson was wrong in everything but the admonishing part of his prophecy,—
that which related to the fate of the rebellion, and that was enough for
the time being.

The *Monitor* was a small affair in comparison with the *Virginia*, and
the work on that vessel was commenced in October 1861, when the *Virginia* was well on toward completion.

During the first days of March a fleet had concentrated near Fortress
Monroe, within cannon shot of the point of egress at which the *Virginia*
was to come forth, the mouth of the Elizabeth River [at Norfolk]. It was
quite a fleet, too. The best vessels [of the Union] were there, to wit: the
Minnesota and the *Roanoke*, intended as twin vessels of the *Virginia* when
they were constructed; also such sailing frigates as the *Cumberland*,
twenty-four guns; the *Congress*, fifty guns; and the *St. Lawrence*, fifty
guns. In view of the possibility of an attack by the *Virginia*, it certainly
seems strange that sailing vessels were allowed in that near vicinity, but it
was no doubt believed that the guns of Fortress Monroe, under which
they should have been but were not, would prove sufficient protection.

[The Federals] had become somewhat careless, commencing to look
upon the *Virginia* as a naval bogy of the seas, a *Flying Dutchman* affair. . . .
The remainder of the [Federal] fleet was at Roanoke [Island, North Carolina,] with General Burnside, and Admiral Goldsborough was there with
it. Captain [John] Marston remained in command of the fleet in the
waters of Fortress Monroe.

"We are tired of waiting for the *Virginia*," wrote Captain [Gershom]
Van Brunt of the *Minnesota*, "and wish she would come out." And she
came out under command of Captain Franklin Buchanan, late of the
United States Navy.

It was high noon on the 8th of March; eight bells had sounded
almost simultaneously on all the shipping in [Hampton] Roads when the
barricades of the Elizabeth River swung open to allow the *Virginia* and
her two tugs to enter the bay. The weather was just right for a fight.

It was the first time that the Confederate ironclad floated upon the
seas, her trial trip so to speak, and she fired a broadside of blank ammunition to announce that she was ready for the fray. The battle was on at
once, for the *Congress*, then at anchor near the mouth of the river, not
over 500 yards from the shore, hailed the Southern vessel with a
broadside at 300 yards. It had no more effect on the ironclad than has
a mosquito bite on the back of a turtle; the broadside was returned
with a single 100-pound rifle shot, which demoralized the *Congress*

considerably. Giving ample time to the *Congress* to raise her anchor, for she was anchored at the time of the *Virginia's* appearance, the *Virginia* proceeded for the *Cumberland,* which was afloat some 200 yards farther down. The *Cumberland* fired at a rapid rate from pivot guns and broadsides, and the *Virginia* with bow on at full speed and without firing a single gun or showing a man, the Bars and Stars alone floating from the main, sent her ram in the Yankee ship below the waterline.

In less than forty minutes the *Cumberland* sunk in some fifty feet of water, but she fired to the very last. Only a few shots were fired by the *Virginia,* and when Captain Buchanan saw his opponent sink he ceased firing. When nothing of the *Cumberland* remained visible but the Stars and Stripes floating from the main just above the waters, the *Virginia* went back to finish the *Congress,* which by this time had raised anchor.

It was not an even fight at all, as no man on board the *Virginia* could be seen, or hurt unless the shot happened to enter a porthole. She took a position within 150 yards of the ill-fated vessel, then aground, and raked her fore and aft until every gun on the *Congress* was dismounted, nearly all the crew killed, including her commander, and by four o'clock the colors were hauled down. The *Congress* had become a slaughter pen, the men fighting as mad against an invisible enemy. The vessel would have been sunk by its men with the Stars and Stripes floating on the main, had she not been fast aground. All the wounded being removed, she was put afire, and by eight o'clock the *Congress* had disappeared, having been blown all to pieces when the fire reached the magazines. . . .

The *Virginia* next set out for her powerful twin sisters, the *Minnesota* and the *Roanoke,* some three miles away, near Fortress Monroe. There was still three hours daylight, and the *Virginia* meant to make her victory complete that day. The *Congress* and the *Cumberland* had ceased to exist, and "fighting Captain Buchanan" meant to finish all [Federal] vessels in Hampton Roads that very evening, and would have done so had not the low water saved them.

The *Minnesota* was stranded. It was impossible for the *Virginia* to reach within a mile of her or she would have been destroyed by the ram as the *Cumberland* had been. The *St. Lawrence* came within reach once, but only once; a shot of the *Virginia's* pivot gun convinced her commander that his vessel was no match for such an enemy, the shot having penetrated near her waterline, doing terrible damage. To save the vessel her commander allowed it to drift down the Roads.

The *Virginia* could not get near the *Minnesota,* but kept firing and doing much damage; but the two small Rebel tugs were enabled to get near the big ship and did considerable damage in killed and wounded, suffering greatly themselves. But the tide kept receding, and at seven o'clock, when darkness had almost set in, the *Virginia* and her tugs pulled off toward the sheltering shores of the Elizabeth River.

Not a shot had penetrated the *Virginia*, although struck a hundred times or more, and not a man was hurt except Captain Buchanan, wounded near the elbow by a rifle bullet fired from the shore by [Federal] men while he was on the roof of his casemate attending to the removal of the wounded sailors on board the *Congress*.[3] [Federal] losses in killed and wounded was nearly three hundred.

The *Roanoke* and *St. Lawrence* were not in reach on account of low water, or they too would certainly have met the same fate as the *Congress* and the *Cumberland*. Captain Van Brunt of the *Minnesota* said that if the *Virginia* had been able to reach the vessel while it was fast aground it would surely have been lost.

But not far away, within the sound of the heavy guns' firing, the [Federal ironclad] *Monitor*, under Commander J. L. Worden, was coming down full speed from New York. Her commander, spurred by the sound of that firing, came as quickly as possible to take part in the fight, and he reached Fortress Monroe at nine o'clock that night, two hours after the *Virginia* had retired from the field of action.

What joy for the sailors on the remaining vessels, and the army on the shore nearby to know that another ironclad had arrived on the scene to meet the one that had played such havoc with the Americans during the day. And well indeed might they rejoice. To be cooped up in a vessel, exposed to the very direst disaster, unable to strike the foe in its vital parts, seeing themselves doomed to destruction without being able to strike at all, is indeed a terrible situation. Stranded on sandbars, a living target for the powerful guns of the enemy was again to be the fate of the *Minnesota* on the next day.

The *Monitor* had come, and with it the night, which enabled [Federal] men to attend to their wounds, repair such damages as were reparable, and to rest after their titanic day's work. Commander Worden was ready to meet Captain Buchanan, and at one o'clock on the morning of the 9th he anchored his vessel close to the *Minnesota*, as the champion of the Americans, ready for battle against all comers.

Surely it must have been a night of the very greatest anxiety to the commander of the *Minnesota*, and to the others, for they had seen the *Virginia*'s work and knew their vessels were no match for her. All efforts to set the *Minnesota* afloat had been in vain; she remained fast aground.

The *Monitor* and her crew, on the contrary, were anxious for daylight in order to avenge the disaster of the day before. During the night Captain Buchanan had been advised of the arrival of the *Monitor* by his spies.

At sunrise on the 9th the *Virginia* left her moorings at Sewell Point, and steamed toward the *Minnesota*, still fast aground some two miles from Fortress Monroe, in search of the newcomer.[4] It was Sunday, the weather was beautiful and the waters placid. The *Virginia*, in search of the channel that led to the *Minnesota*, passed right under the guns of Fortress Monroe, not minding their shooting in the least, slowly but steadily nearing her antagonist. But the *Monitor* was on the watch, shielding the *Minnesota* as much as her size would allow. The *Virginia*, without any further ado, opened fiercely on the *Monitor*, hitting her several times, but only once squarely on the turret, the 100-pound rifle shot going halfway through and hurting one man slightly. The *Monitor* answered with her 168-pounder, her only gun, but it had no effect at all upon the *Virginia*.

In the maneuvering for positions, the *Virginia* went aground and the *Monitor*, turning all around her, tried in vain to find a vulnerable spot, but she remained impervious to the 168 pounds of cast iron, the shots glancing off, although the two antagonists almost touched one another. The *Virginia* soon got afloat, and instead of losing her time with the *Monitor* turned all her attention on the *Minnesota*, going bow-on full speed toward the big vessel. However, owing to the low water, she was unable to reach the *Minnesota*, or that vessel would have been pierced by the *Virginia*'s formidable ram.

Seeing the ironclad's advance, the *Minnesota* fired full broadside, every shot hitting the *Virginia* but all to no purpose. The *Virginia* then shelled the *Minnesota* in order to set her afire, but the *Monitor* interfered and before the *Virginia* had fired her fourth shell, literally jumped on the ironclad, which was then compelled to defend herself.

In changing positions the *Virginia* grounded again, and another broadside from the *Minnesota*, with a 168-pounder from the *Monitor*, struck her. She remained invulnerable; it was really useless to fire at her.

Afloat once again, she steamed down the bay for deeper water, closely followed by the *Monitor*. Their speed was about equal. The *Minnesota*, thinking that the *Virginia* fled from the field of action, set up a cheer of victory. It was all too soon, for the *Virginia*, quick as lightning, veered clear around and bounced upon the *Monitor* bow-on, expecting to ram her through, lifting her prow almost out of the water upon her ram. The *Monitor* resisted the shock nobly, and simply slipped off, remaining apparently unharmed. The firing continued for some time until the *Monitor* was seen to retire down the bay toward [Fortress] Monroe.

The *Virginia* once again headed for the *Minnesota*, whose ammunition was almost expended, half her guns dismounted, and the men worn out with fatigue. It was a terrible moment for Captain Van Brunt, who was at a loss to know why the *Monitor* had retired while the *Virginia* was returning to finish her up. But on taking another look at the ironclad soon after, he saw that she had changed her course, and had no intention of keeping up the conflict. The last shot had been fired, the great fight was over, and Van Brunt could breathe easy.

It has been said that when the *Virginia* rammed the *Monitor* and lifted her prow out of the water, the ram was so wrenched by the weight that a leak had sprung, and for that reason the ship had speeded back. Perhaps it was in the repairing of this leak that President Davis became so much interested that he made his regular visits to Norfolk.

Commander Worden [of the *Monitor*] had been wounded in the head and partly blinded; he was obliged to turn over the command of his vessel to Lieutenant [S. Dana] Green. The *Monitor* had one of her pilot-house logs, a piece of iron nine by twelve inches square, shattered to pieces, causing the wound of the commander. . . .

The *Minnesota* after a great deal of work was enabled to reach Fortress Monroe, being most seriously crippled, and having only eleven out of her fifty guns fit for service. The victory evidently belonged to the South so far as prestige was concerned, but it gave her no particular advantages. Had she been able to destroy the *Monitor*, or even able to remain in action, she might have gone to Hatteras Inlet and demolished the fleet of Admiral Goldsborough. Providence was assuredly with [the North].

Captain Buchanan was promoted to admiral after the fight, and the *Virginia* had for her new commander one Josiah Tattnall, a famous veteran of the United States Navy. It is strange indeed that neither the *Virginia* nor the *Monitor* ever again came in contact, and yet for the next two months they were scarcely four miles apart. The would peep at each other occasionally, make feints, and then withdraw to their respective lairs.[5]

Tattnall was a fighter from away back, and seeing that his vessel was going to be shut up in the Elizabeth River in case Norfolk was evacuated, he asked leave to proceed to Yorktown to destroy the American fleet at that place or perish in the attempt. The secretary of the Confederate navy refused him permission.

And so when Norfolk was being evacuated, unable to take his vessel up the James River, Tattnall determined to destroy her to keep her out of Federal hands. Accordingly he scuttled the *Virginia* and blew her up; not a vestige of it remained.

That was the [11th] of May [1862], and he then sent word to Richmond: "The *Virginia* has ceased to exist. I presume that a court of inquiry will be ordered to examine into the circumstances, and I earnestly solicit it. Public opinion will never be put right without it."[6]

A court of inquiry being appointed, it found that the destruction of the *Virginia* was not necessary under the circumstances, and a court-martial was convened to try Commander Tattnall. He was honorably acquitted because he had asked permission to go to meet the enemy but had been refused to do so. He later retired to his famous estate in Georgia, one of the finest in the world, where many soldiers of the 7th Army Corps passed many pleasant hours during the Spanish American War while in camp at Savannah.

CHAPTER 20

Last Day in Richmond

But what of this man John Walker; what was he about? This was a question that concerned our friends very much, and to which they were giving attention. It is probable that the evacuation of Fredericksburg by General Smith and its occupation by General McDowell was the cause of his leaving home, as would seem quite natural. But the change in his personal appearance, and his being frequently seen by the Frenchmen, was not so easily explained.

They had paid him a liberal price for his horses, two of which he most likely got back after the Aquia Creek surprise; he could have no cause for complaints against them unless for the somewhat summary manner in which he had been treated when he parted with the horses. This probably he would never forget, nor forgive; the idea that such Yankee youngsters made him jump about, just as he made his slaves. He was a most intense Rebel.

One day while wandering about the streets of Richmond, Walker saw all three of the Frenchmen, but they never noticed him. He at once took steps to discover where they lived, and from that time he dogged their footsteps. Having disguised his personal appearance he felt safe from detection. He soon discovered that they were chaperoned a great deal by the provost marshal of Richmond; that they lived with Major Denson, an important government official; and that they had plenty of money, coming and going as they pleased, when and where they chose.

All this was enough to excite the curiosity of John Walker, and made him quite suspicious. There was a mystery in it which he meant to unravel, and now that he had seen them purchase horses, he became still more anxious. He was an extremely dangerous man, very vindictive, extremely bitter. As D'Artagnan never paid any attention to him, he was convinced that his disguise was complete, and that all he had to do was to bide his time until he could make up a plan of vengeance.

Our friends had come to the positive conclusion that they would not pay any attention to John Walker so long as they were in Richmond; that they would go their own way as usual, taking a ride every day and always on the same pike, which was the Gordonsville Road. John Walker soon found this out, and never followed them, convinced that they were simply out for a ride.

But he had determined to follow them when they left the city for good, knowing that they would soon do so, as he was told by the proprietor of the stable that the gentlemen wanted his very best horses "for the reason that they had a long journey before them, and money did not seem to be much of a consideration with them, and they were the very best judges of horseflesh he ever saw." Walker knew the truth of the last assertion to his sorrow. No matter what good things he heard of the young Frenchmen, John Walker was convinced that they were suspicious characters, and he meant to investigate.

It was the 9th of May, and while talking in their rooms, the Frenchmen would hear the booming of the guns more distinctly than ever. Williamsburg is only some forty miles southeast of Richmond, and as that was the rainy season the wind carried the sound directly towards them.

"What do you think of it, Athos?" asked D'Artagnan.

"I think that the Federals are advancing slowly, but steadily. Williamsburg is untenable, and Longstreet will withdraw and fall back until he will reach some opportune line of defence more effective for him than forts, which can be attacked by gunboats and surrounded with troops.[1] I saw in the paper this morning that General Lee and Mr. Davis were looking along the Chickahominy for the next line of defence. If driven from that line, the Confederates will be compelled to evacuate Richmond at an early day; if on the contrary they drive our army back, Richmond is safe for some time, as the approaches on the left bank of the James River are strengthened with permanent fortifications. You can from this window catch a glimpse of the left bank, and with these glasses I have seen the work progressing there. I do not believe it is over four miles away."

"Well, if we have to get out of this we have good horses to carry us, and I for my part would not be sorry to shake Richmond dust from my feet. Surely we cannot complain of the manner in which we have been treated, and Providence has been extremely kind to us, but as far as we are concerned this is not war; still, it has been dangerous enough. I dare say, however, I care less for danger when I can do my share of the fighting."

"The same with me," said Aramis,

The latter had been in dreamland for the last few days. He had made more visits to Miss Alice late in the evening. He had told her who he was, and being absolutely sure of her love, he had told her his object in coming to Richmond. She was terrified at the idea, but did not blame him. In her eyes he could do no wrong,—what he did must be right.

However, knowing who he and his friends were, she became anxious for their safety, wishing them to depart as soon as possible and return to their friends until Richmond would be taken. It had been agreed that at the very first opportunity he would take her to France where she would be among the first ladies of the land in social standing. The last night he remained in Richmond, they pledged one another's troths, and he gave her an engagement ring which she promised to keep until death ensued.

The morning papers announced the evacuation of Williamsburg and the withdrawal of all Confederate troops from Norfolk. The city was to be entirely evacuated that day, the navy yard and the *Virginia* being doomed to destruction. The last hope was gone. . . .

"Well," said D'Artagnan to his friends after having read the news in the morning papers, "we must make ready to leave. You have noticed the uneasy feeling among the people, running here, running there; you can see from here quantities of packing boxes, full of archives probably, around the capitol opposite us, ready to be shipped to some place of safety.[2] When shall we go our way to Gordonsville and liberty?"

"Let us leave tomorrow morning."

"Very well, at eight o'clock, horseback, and adieu to Richmond. This day let us pay a visit to Secretary Benjamin and Captain Alexander, and finish all that we have to do here."

Mr. Benjamin received them kindly, and when he was informed that they would leave in the morning, he expressed his sorrow and wished them a pleasant journey. . . . The parting of Captain Alexander was the parting of friends. D'Artagnan took occasion on this visit to present the captain, on behalf of himself and his friends, a most valuable ring, as a token of their esteem and thanks for his great kindness to them while they were in dire distress.

That evening a terrible explosion was heard. The navy yard at Norfolk was being destroyed, and the *Virginia* had fired her last shot in blowing herself to pieces.[3] Not enough of her remained together to enable [Federal] engineers to discover the secret of her construction and power.

That same evening D'Artagnan told Major Denson that they would leave in the morning and asked leave to bid farewell to the ladies before departing.

"Now then," said he when back in his room, "what are we going to do with the extra stuff that has accumulated here in the way of clothes and linens? It would take a small trunk to hold all that, and we cannot be encumbered with it."

"We could ask the major to allow us to give it to the servants," said Athos, "and we can purchase what we may be in need of on the way, and throw away what we are done with. The narcotics I have dropped in the sink at the hotel."

"We ought, I think, to dress in the same clothes we wore when we reached here," said Aramis, "so that we may not be looked upon as Rebels when we get in the vicinity of our men."

"That goes without saying," said D'Artagnan, "and I feel very happy over our early departure. We have failed to do what we intended, and I much regret it, but it is not our fault. It was a big scheme, and Mr. Davis's good luck saved him. I have thought of other plans,—I have racked my brain to hit one that would enable us to dispose of Davis, but short of death I have found none. That is not to be thought of. We will risk our lives for an honorable deed, but cold-blooded murder will not do."

"Which way are we going?"

"Direct to Gordonsville to begin with, thence according to circumstances, but the shortest way towards the Federal pickets. I have a good chart in my pocket; the road is marked upon it to Gordonsville, thence to Knoxville, thence to Nashville. Of course this is only for appearance sake; I might get shot and have pockets rifled. Every night we will consult over the point to be reached next day. Captain Alexander will see us off in the morning I am sure, although we bade him good-bye, and we may ask him for form's sake what place to strike after Gordonsville, but we shall decide for ourselves which way to go."

Aramis found his way to the Densons' parlor that evening. The door was wide open, as usual, and the lights burned brightly. A death-like silence pervaded the surroundings. Alice greeted him on the threshold, but more warmly this time than ever before. It was to be the last time. She threw her arms around his neck and kissed him, breaking into tears.

"The last time, my Maurice; tomorrow you will be far away! My thoughts will follow you, and I shall pray God that He may lead you safely through all danger, and will always pray, "Oh, my God, return him to me!". . .

"Dear, dear Alice!"

"Now let me tell you before I am too much overcome. You must go to Gordonsville; thence to Orange Court House, whence you may inquire from the negroes (your only reliable friends here) where the Federal pickets are. Father told me he thought they were on the left bank of the Rapidan.

"I have a very dear friend near Orange Court House, one mile west of the place. Here is a note to her. It will prove an asylum. . . . It is only a short while ago that she was here with me, and she said, 'Alice, I must go. I would die here seeing the spirit of hate that permeates the hearts of men and women.'"

Alice continued, "I would ask my parents to let me go with you to see her, if it were not for their very poor state of health," and her eyes filled with tears. "They cannot live long, and I will soon be all alone with Minnie, unless you come back to me, or I be allowed to go to you."

"Do not speak thus, dear girl, or I will not be able to leave."

"Then father also says, in the Shenandoah Valley the Federal pickets are near Columbia Bridge. You and your friends can trust my friend Miss Stannard at Orange Court House. I have written her about you. If you had her for a guide,—she is born there,—you would be safe. I led her to believe, however, that you were going to your cousin, the Prince de Polignac, and that you were noncombatants. You can reach her in less than two days. Do you remember the directions?"

"Yes, Orange Court House, one mile west, Miss Maud Stannard."

"Yes."

"I have made arrangements with the French consul by which you can hear from me, and I from you; briefly, it is true, but our hearts will supply the rest."

"Now, Maurice, my friend Maud is as pretty as she is sweet, and . . ."

"Not another word, my Alice. You will fill my whole heart forever." Laughingly he added, "And you forget that my two friends are not disciples of St. Anthony!"[4]

They remained together longer than usual, and their parting made two hearts ache with intense grief.

CHAPTER 21

Away from Richmond

THE MORNING WAS BEAUTIFUL. THE HORSES WERE LED TO THE house on Capitol Square, and Captain Alexander, as D'Artagnan had guessed he would be, was at hand riding his own charger.

The major and his wife were bidden a kind farewell, so was Alice who had tears in her eyes, and whose heart throbbed in agony though she dared not sob outright. All three Frenchmen kissed a sweet good-bye to little Minnie, and away they went.

"Fine young men," said Major Denson, "what a pity they will not fight for us."

Mrs. Denson looked at her daughter and at once guessed what the trouble was with Alice, and must have muttered to herself, "Poor girl!"

Alice was still at the door when the rest of the family had left, gazing on the departing ones, and following one with all her heart. A last farewell with their hands, and the inflexible street corner that parted them from each other's view, perhaps forever.

Someone else watched all this. [John] Walker was some distance away in the street. He returned to the stable with the proprietor, who had come with the horses to see that everything was all right, and whom he accosted.

"Are those young fellows going away?"

"Yes, they are bound for Mississippi by the way of Gordonsville, Knoxville, and Nashville."

"If it were not for those regular Virginia straw hats, I would take them for Yanks with their swords and pistols in the holsters."

"Yes, they do look like Yanks, but they are not. They are Frenchmen, and the French are our friends. Moreover, I fancy by the way in which they handle their horses that they can use both sword and pistol as well as the next."

"No doubt."

Our party kept on a walk in the city, and the people looked with some surprise at those semi-Federal young men accompanied by Captain Alexander in his Confederate uniform. He was riding ahead with D'Artagnan, and Aramis came next with Athos. Both the latter had bowed a last farewell to Miss Alice, and Athos could see tears in Aramis's eyes, and said: "Aha, my dear Aramis, this sweet Southern maiden has you by the strings of the heart in dead earnest. Upon my soul, she is worthy of a kingdom, and she will make you as beautiful and sweet a duchess as you can find."

Aramis gave him a grateful but sad look, and said, "If she does not, no other ever will."

They soon reached the gates of the city, where owing to the presence of the captain no questions were asked, and they soon found themselves on the beautiful pike that leads to Gordonsville. The leaves were out nearly in full on the trees planted at regular intervals along the side of the road, all carefully and regularly trimmed. The road might have been taken for a beautiful avenue in some well-regulated park.

"I have ordered breakfast for four at the Relay House, some ten miles from here," said Captain Alexander. "Before the war it was a place of great resort, and it is not bad now. It may probably be the last time we shall meet around the festive board, and we will trust to luck for the future."

"Captain," said Aramis, "I have your promise that after this war you will be my guest in Paris. How long do you think this war is going to last, anyway?"

"We mean to fight to the last, that is to say until the South is recognized as an independent state. We shall exhaust our whole strength to that effect."

"It is really terrible," said Athos, "to see such a beautiful country, possessing all that is necessary to make it the greatest nation on earth, given up to and torn by fratricidal civil war."

"Don't let us talk of this very sad and serious matter. What is the name of the horse dealer who sold us these horses?"

"Jerome, he is of French origin."

"Well, let us give Jerome's horses a trial."

Away they went at a rapid pace. The horses were perfect, high-spirited, but well trained. Along the road they met a couple of regiments on their way to Richmond. They were told that they belonged to General Jackson's army and were going to swell General Lee's forces, but that they would be returned at once if it were found that they were not needed there, as a movement northward by Jackson, known as Stonewall, was intended that month.

"Here we are," said the captain, "let us go in. I am glad to see the place deserted; we shall be more at our ease. Well, what do you think of your mounts?"

"I think," said D'Artagnan, looking at them, "that they are good for a long trip; not a hair seems to be turned, and we have ridden the last nine miles in little less than an hour's time, and these turnpikes I take to be hard roads for the horses."

The hostlers led the horses away towards the stable, and the riders went in. "By the way," called D'Artagnan after the departing hostlers, "only a little water just now, but plenty of hay. Give them their oats in half an hour."

The grounds of the Relay House were very large and beautifully laid out with yew trees, and though they seemed to be somewhat neglected just then, the general appearance was very good, considering that not very far away from there, two mighty armies were marshalling their forces to meet in a long and fierce onslaught. Then, too, one-half of the slaves within a circuit of forty miles from Richmond were working at the fortifications on the north bank of the James River, and the proprietor of the Relay House, having furnished his quota, was short the hands necessary to keep his place in its usual condition.

The house was three-story, of stone, located about one hundred yards from the pike. The rooms were airy and cool; it seemed to be a delightful place for the Southern gentry to while away their spare time.

An excellent breakfast was served.

At parting, Captain Alexander told his friends that they could easily make Louisa Court House by sundown. He advised them to stop at some plantation instead of at an inn where they were likely to come in [contact] with the military. "Let me hear from you if possible," and he returned to Richmond.

"It is too bad," said Athos, "to deceive such a fine fellow, and I feel somewhat sorry for so doing. It was, however, out of all reason to tell him our story."

We have done him no harm, anyway, and he would, after all, find our deception quite natural after learning what we were about,—if ever he does," said D'Artagnan. "Do you know, I feel like a new man just now, just as I felt when we left Manassas Junction, and if we do get into trouble, our horses will soon take us out of harm's reach, if discretion is to be the better part of valor."

Instead of stopping east of Louisa Court Hose, they went one mile west, and passed the night at a beautiful plantation, whose owners were all gone, and the overseer in charge of the slaves did the honors of the place.

D'Artagnan took pains to find out all about Gordonsville from the slaves as there was not a white man to be seen about the place. From these he learned that the Confederate troops had been there in large numbers, and that as a rule they were quartered upon the citizens, that they were a deal of trouble, and some of them very, very wild.

Now, as before when they were on the road to Richmond before being captured by Colonel Lee, they arranged their plans at night for the following day.

"I have not told you," said Aramis to his friends, "that Miss Alice gave me a letter to a friend of hers living one mile west of Orange Court House, and requested me to stop there."

"Miss Alice is indeed a most charming and useful quartermaster," said Athos, "but where is Orange Court House? Take your map out, D'Artagnan."

"She said we ought to reach there in a day and a half."

"Yes," said D'Artagnan looking on his chart, "it is some ten miles north of Gordonsville. We had better leave the pike before reaching that place and take an ordinary road leading to Orange Court House. It will be somewhat longer to travel, but it may save us trouble. Of course, if any questions are asked as to our destination, we are on our way to Knoxville. I do not anticipate any trouble, however, unless we are tackled by some meddlesome officers or surly troopers."

An hour before sunset on the second day out of Richmond they found themselves at Mr. Stannard's plantation. It was an imposing looking place, but to all appearance it was almost deserted. The residence was not far from the road and, surrounded by clusters of big beautiful trees, was almost hidden from view. The barking of a dog gave them a direction in which to go.

The house was a Colonial style as so many are in that part of the country. The dog that had been barking kept them at bay within a reasonable distance from the house. It was a large and beautiful St. Bernard, with shaggy hair and of yellowish color. As it was either a case of dog jumping on man, or man jumping on dog, the horsemen came to a standstill, the faithful watch kept sounding the alarm, until finally some one appeared on the portico to pacify him, when he fell back upon the one who had ordered him to desist.

"You may approach now."

"You have the note, Aramis," said D'Artagnan, "go to meet the lady."

She was a beautiful young woman of commanding appearance. Athos and D'Artagnan remained in place, and Aramis dismounted, handing his reins to D'Artagnan while he proceeded towards the fair mistress of the place, raising his hat.

"Good evening, Madam. I beg pardon for disturbing your solitude at this time of day, but we are looking for the home of Mr. Stannard."

"This is the place, sir."

"Is Miss Maud Stannard about the premises?"

"I am Maud Stannard, and if I mistake not, I know who you and the gentlemen yonder are."

Aramis smiled.

"Then all that I have to do is hand you this note, with the compliments of Miss Alice Denson of Richmond," and he presented the note.

Strange as it may seem, the huge dog had approached Aramis, and was kindly wagging his tail while touching Aramis's hand with his cold muzzle.

Aramis had forgotten all about the dog while conversing with Miss Maud, and was much startled at feeling the splendid animal touching his hand, but he simply laid it on the dog's head and patted it, while Miss Maud read the note. She raised her eyes to Aramis, and to her great surprise saw her dog near him.

"Do not be afraid, sir. Come here, Lion. I have never seen him act that way before."

Aramis smiled, saying: "Go, good Lion. You have a noble dog there, Miss Maud; a faithful guardian."

"But pardon me," she said, "I will call one of the servants to take care of your horses. And you, gentlemen, please come near."

She went in, and very soon a darky of the very blackest hue came to hold the horses. Lion had returned to Aramis.

"My faithful guardian, as you call him, is to all appearances ready to desert me," said Miss Maud on her return to the porch. . . .

"We are grateful to you, Miss, for your kindness, and we hope that we are not intruding upon your good nature," said D'Artagnan.

"Not in the least, on the contrary, I would feel aggrieved if you were not to wait until Father's return. When did you leave Richmond?"

"Yesterday morning."

"Have you seen many soldiers on the way there?"

"No, we were advised by Captain Alexander to keep out of the town of Gordonsville; so we took country lanes as we approached that place, and we have seen but a few soldiers."

"You know we are in great dread of small parties; they help themselves with the greatest freedom to all horses they can lay their hands on, and we have but three left. My father has gone to Orange to secure a guard for us."

"Are there no men around this place?"

"My father is the only one; I have two brothers in the army. Father is getting old and feeble and cannot cope with the young men that are giving us the trouble. The brother of Lion is chained in the stable, and I keep as good watch as I can."

"Well," said D'Artagnan, who had kept up the conversation, "this is really too bad, and I am surprised that the authorities allow such a state of affairs."

In reality he was not much surprised at learning this, for he was well aware how soldiers made themselves easy with horseflesh when it was required. He and his friends had once found themselves in the same dilemma, but had paid for the horses, and it is safe to say that if a lady had been about the stable of John Walker, they would have walked their way rather than compel her father or husband to part with them against their wishes.

Miss Maud was sitting near the window.

"Ah," said she, "here is my father; pray excuse me for a moment," and she walked out to meet him.

Very soon she returned, preceded by a gentleman well advanced in years, with long white hair like cavaliers of old, rather feeble, leaning on a cane. He was of Huguenot origin and French descent as his name indicated.[1] The visitors were introduced to him by his daughter as the French gentlemen of whom her friend Miss Denson had written. He addressed them in French, which he spoke as well as any born Frenchman, thinking that they were not familiar with the English language.

"You are welcome, gentlemen, and I am happy to see you. It is nearly one hundred years ago that my grandfather came over with Lafayette. After the war was over he settled right here, and made it one of the handsomest places in Virginia."

"But Papa," said Miss Maud, "you forget that I do not speak French well enough to follow a conversation. The gentlemen speak English very well."

"Oh, I beg your pardon, dear. I will speak English."

Our friends, with their hats in hand, had remained standing. The old gentleman bade them to be seated.

"Maud, call a servant and tell him to care for the hats of those gentlemen. It is growing late, and if you are not obliged to follow your journey this evening, I beg you to accept my hospitality."

"Mr. Stannard," said D'Artagnan, "if we can do so without inconveniencing you, we will accept your kind invitation with the greatest pleasure. We are total strangers in these parts, and would have trouble in finding an inn."

"Our solitude is very great here just now, and we are pleased to have company. We are troubled with a disagreeable set of visitors now and then, whom we cannot receive in the house,—private soldiers of the regiments moving about, who leave their commands to maraude and rob. I have just been to Orange to secure a guard, but the provost marshal guard that was there has been removed, and I shall have to go all the way to General Ewell's headquarters at Fort Republic to secure one.[2]

"These are very troublesome times," continued Stannard. "My sons are gone to the army and have been away nearly one year; they are at Yorktown and, as I understand it, are falling back on Williamsburg and Chickahominy probably. Strange to say, and I am ashamed to say it, but the Federals have reconnoitered here and they never disturbed anything. It is not over two weeks ago that a whole regiment of cavalry, coming from across the Rapidan, moving westward passed here, and I have not heard a single complaint."

"I dare say that marauders of the Federal army would receive very cold comfort here, as they should, for this is for them the enemy's country."

Miss Maud had closely observed the strangers during the time, and had no doubt come to the conclusion that her friend Alice had very good taste indeed, but that it differed from hers. She presently left the room to give orders to the servants to have rooms ready for the guests, and to attend to such matters as her duty of housekeeper required of her.

"Now, gentlemen," said Stannard, "please go to the stable and see that your horses are carefully attended to by the hostlers just as you wish them to be. I am too feeble to accompany you."

They went, and Lion followed Aramis as he would a master of years' standing. It was indeed strange, that sudden affection for a total stranger, but it was not a new thing to Aramis. Following their horses, in charge of the negro who had them in hand, they soon reached the stable, which they thought was too far from the house, and they decided that one of them would be on watch during the night.

Entering the stable they were greeted by another huge St. Bernard with a growl that meant nothing good for them if in reach of him. But Lion being with them, he very soon became peaceful, and before leaving the stable they had ceased to be strangers to him. The visitors watched those two magnificent animals gambol and play together, in silent admiration. It was difficult for them to say which was which, and when they left the stable, Lion following them, Tiger entered a plaintive protest at not being permitted to accompany them.

They strolled over the grounds, admiring the beautiful trees and well laid-out avenues of yews, until a servant approached informing them that dinner was waiting.

Miss Maud was a beautiful blonde, some twenty-two years of age, of very stately figure, much of the same character as Miss Alice, who was a brunette. To the old gentleman and the young lady, this must have been one of the most agreeable evenings they had enjoyed for a long time.

Aramis's thoughts were in Richmond; he was quieter than usual. Athos and D'Artagnan kept up the conversation, and in so doing greatly pleased and interested their hosts. Lion was a privileged character, lying close to Aramis, who said to Mr. Stannard: "Those dogs of yours are really splendid animals. I have never seen finer ones and I have some rare ones of the same type at home."

"They were pups when I bought them at the monastery at St. Bernard in 1859. They are brothers, and strangers always have trouble in distinguishing one from another. They are exceedingly well-trained; they will eat nothing unless it comes from their regular keeper or direct from the hands of a friend. Just now one or the other is always kept chained in the stable during the daytime, but loose in it at night, and a faithful servant sleeps in the barn. You notice that my stable is of stone, and is locked from the inside every night. The dog at night will never bark unless he scents a stranger lurking about the stable, and when he does give the alarm, we have to be on the lookout. There will be a fight before any more horses are stolen from my barn."

"How many have you lost?"

"Three. You see the stable is some distance from the house, thus encouraging evildoers, and I have been obliged to take steps to guard the premises. I think that they are well guarded now, for I am sure that no one can come very near without the alarm being given. Nevertheless, I will go to the city tomorrow to see if I can secure a guard, and if you are in no particular hurry to proceed on your journey I will deem it a favor on your part to give us at least one more day of your company, as I do not like to leave my daughter alone for a whole day in these exasperating times."

"If agreeable to you and Miss Maud, we shall deem it a pleasure as well as a duty to remain," said Athos. "Our time has no limit just now; we are traveling as tourists and at the grace of God."

It was getting late, and the old gentleman and his daughter retired, leaving the Frenchmen to pass the remainder of the evening to their leisure. Immediately after the Stannards' departure a servant entered the room, informing them that Miss Maud had told him to put himself at their disposal. He was asked to conduct them to the smoking room, which he did. Then they told him to return in about an hour to be shown to their rooms.

"Well," said D'Artagnan after they were comfortably seated, enjoying their cigars, "we are not so far from our lines just now. Not twenty miles. But before cutting loose we need much information which we have to secure from the negroes, and they are not oversmart."

"Why not ask Miss Maud?"

"She is too intelligent. I'll let you do the talking with her, Athos, and I will talk with the negroes."

"And so will I," said Aramis.

"Why, what's the matter with you, Aramis? Are you going to do penance for your happy days in Richmond?"

"Never mind, Athos," was the reply, as Aramis went out to finish his cigar under the beautiful oaks and elms around the residence, Lion at his heels.

"I think," said D'Artagnan to Athos, "that we had better go straight from here to Conrad's Store, some fifteen miles distant. General Ewell is near Fort Republic with his division, and Conrad's Store is some twelve miles north of that. With a negro guide we could possibly get through some gap in the mountains and across the Rebel lines. This we shall have to look up tomorrow, so as to be ready to move at any time."

When Aramis returned from his walk he stated that everything was quiet and peaceful; that he had gone near the stables and had heard nothing there.

CHAPTER 22

Fight at the Mansion

THE NEXT MORNING MR. STANNARD STARTED FOR GORDONSVILLE, AND agreeable to their promise, our friends remained his guests.

D'Artagnan took a ride in the morning, hoping to see some darky who might be able to give him news as to the whereabouts of the Federal picket lines. The only information he secured was that on the north side of the Rapidan [River] the Yankees might be met at any time, and that west of the Shenandoah River it was a regular deadline, where one was as liable to be shot by a Yank as by a Rebel, all the way from Fort Republic to New Market.

He did not meet a single white man during his ride nor over half a dozen blacks, and was returning to the Stannard mansion by a round-about way that took him near Orange Court House. He had left his sword in his room, but carried a pistol. Between Orange and the mansion he saw a man on horseback, riding the same direction as he was, overtaking him he recognized John Walker.

"How are you, Mr. Walker?" he said with a sarcastic smile. "Pray what may you be doing in these parts?"

One may well imagine the surprise of the Virginian, who, greatly disconcerted as he must have been, never allowed it to be seen.

"May I inquire your name, sir?"

"Is it possible that you do not recognize me, my dear Mr. Walker? I bought some horses from you some five or six weeks ago."

"You certainly mistake, sir; I do not know that I have ever seen you before."

"So, so," thought D'Artagnan, "the rascal is more dangerous than I believed," and he restrained an impulse to take the man by the nape of the neck and shake him off his horse. But he wisely concluded to play the same part Walker was playing.

"Then I must be strangely mistaken, for I would have sworn you were John Walker, a farmer living a few miles from Occoquan, who committed perjury to secure the arrest of three young men whom he took for Yankees; in short, John Walker, a number-one scoundrel."

All this time D'Artagnan kept his eyes on him, but not a muscle of Walker's face revealed any sign of fear or of anger; he remained impossible to insult. The Frenchman was at a loss to know what to do. He remained as self-possessed as the Virginian himself, and had spoken as insultingly as he could, hoping to anger Walker to the point of hostility. But all in vain.

"Well, sir, I hope you will pardon my mistake, and rejoice that you are not the rascal I suspected you of being. I bid you good morning."

By this time the two had reached the gate of the Stannard mansion, and D'Artagnan rode in. His two friends were in the avenue leading to the residence, and could easily be seen from the road. Walker must have seen them.

"Who was that fellow riding with you?" asked Athos.

"That is John Walker, and as he did not want to be recognized I did not insist, thinking that if I did so, there would surely be a dead Walker on the road, and we really cannot afford it just now."

"But he surely recognized you; he must have seen us, and may concoct some scheme that will delay us."

"Of course; he is not here for his health. He has followed us from Richmond, probably lost our track and would not have known where we were, had I not met him. He was riding slowly when I first saw him, and as he could not possibly have known that we were stopping here, he certainly must have believed that he had lost us.

I gave him a piece of my mind that will not make him feel more kindly toward us, and he is no doubt bent on giving us more trouble, the very thing that we desire to avoid, now that we are near our picket lines. Athos, please see Miss Maud right away and ask her where the nearest military post is to be found. I take it that he will go there and report that he saw three Yankees here."

"Well, suppose he does?"

"It is probable that a squad of soldiers will be sent here to look us up."

"We have our passes."

"True, but this fellow may put up some story that will cause an investigation of some kind or other, and as a consequence, cause delay."

Walker had indeed lost all hope of finding the Frenchmen, and was on the point of giving up the search when D'Artagnan had overtaken him on the road. The roasting that he then received had as a matter of course increased his hatred, and he at once determined to go to the nearest camp to report the presence of several Yankees near Orange Court House. The first negro met by Walker told him there was a regiment of cavalry in camp near Conrad's Store, about ten miles away, and there he intended to go. But his horse was nearly worn out, and his progress was slow.

Miss Maud told Athos that the nearest camp was at Conrad's Store, and when the latter told D'Artagnan about it, he at once decided to go there and report in person to the commanding officer. As he had not yet dismounted from his horse he was ready to go.

"In case you see Walker coming back this way, do not be surprised; let him go. I have a plan."

He started at full speed and caught up with Walker at a short distance. The latter turned around to see who was riding so fast behind him, and recognized his man at once. It was impossible for him to make his horse go any faster, so he jogged along as best he could. D'Artagnan soon caught up with him, and relaxing the speed of his horse, as he went by he said, "John Walker, I will tell them that you are coming, that you are a most dangerous scoundrel, and that they had better take hold of you as soon as you put in an appearance. I will then swear out a warrant against you for perjury and that will settle you for some time. *Au revoir*, John Walker."

D'Artagnan gave the reins to his horse and resumed his speed.

Walker was in a dilemma. He knew that he had sworn falsely, that it was so admitted at the provost marshal general's office in Richmond, and that it could be proven. He instinctively put his hand to his pistol with a desire to kill, but was afraid to attempt it.

"That young devil of a Frenchman! He is liable to get me into serious trouble if I do not look out. What shall I do? Oh, if I were only sure of my aim."

On his arrival at Conrad's Store D'Artagnan was stopped by a sentinel, and he asked to be conducted to the commanding officer; so he was.

"Colonel, here is a pass that explains itself. Myself and two friends are stopping at Mr. Stannard's, a few miles from here, for a day or so. I have deemed it best to advise you of our presence there so that you may not be misled."

"How is it that you are stopping there?"

"We had a letter for Miss Stannard from a friend of hers in Richmond, the daughter of Major Denson of the Ordnance Department. Mr.

Stannard left this morning for General Ewell's headquarters to ask for a provost guard, as he is troubled very much with marauders and hangers-on; he asked us to stay at his place until his return."

"You said Major Denson, I believe?"

"Yes, Colonel; we stopped with him some three weeks."

"I know the major well; how is he and his family?"

"He and his wife seem to be in feeble health; Miss Alice and her younger sister are well, very well."

"You see that I am on the move, or I would go to Mr. Stannard with you. I will be back here during the night. Good day, sir."

With the exception of a camp guard, the colonel with his regiment already in saddle when D'Artagnan arrived moved northward at a brisk trot. Our Frenchman at once took the road for the Stannard mansion and expected to meet Walker on the way, but failed to see anything of him. As he returned by the road on which he had come, it was evident that the Virginian, scared by what D'Artagnan had told him, had gone back or taken some other road leading to Fort Republic.

"The rascal is good enough to shoot me from some hidden place," thought D'Artagnan. I had better have my pistol ready." He drew it from the holster and placed it in his belt, keeping a sharp lookout right and left. . . .

Meanwhile, Athos and Aramis had taken a look at the surroundings of the place. They had a chat with Miss Maud, who was obliged to excuse herself that she might attend to household matters and informed them that she would meet them at luncheon.

"Now Aramis, that young lady who has probably ridden over every foot of this beautiful country should be able to give us some information as to the mountain gaps of which we hear so much. We ought to find out how to cross the Shenandoah. D'Artagnan told me last night while you were rambling about the stable that if we could get across in a northwest-erly direction from here, he felt sure that we could reach our own lines. 'At any rate,' as he said, 'we must take our chances.'"

"Very well, I shall ask Miss Maud. I suppose we can bring up the sub-ject at luncheon. D'Artagnan will probably be back by that time."

D'Artagnan was not back, and they were alone to take their midday meal with Miss Maud, but could not find out anything very satisfactory from her. She told them that John, the stable man who had kept their horses when they arrived, went over the river nearly every Saturday evening to see his wife, a slave over there. He said that sometimes the Confederates were there, and sometimes the Federals.

A horseback ride was suggested by Miss Maud, and orders were given to that effect. Soon after, they were in the saddle, Athos being the young lady's cavalier.

"I will show you over my father's place,—a portion of it anyway. I am always very proud to show it; it is such a lovely home."

It was indeed a magnificent domain, comprising several thousand acres, a large portion of which was timberland, quite hilly in some places. The young lady and Athos had to bear the burden of the conversation, as Aramis was not in the best of moods, thinking that he might have had his Alice here with him had he only known of his staying at the house of her friend. It was, however, too late to think of telling her to come, as on the morrow they would probably leave.

The barking of Tiger at the stable hurried them back to the residence.

"Probably some of those terrible men who at times prowl around and have respect for nothing. I do so fear them. I am told that most of them are deserters. Father hates the very sight of them."

"So long as we are here," said Athos, "you need not have fears, Miss Maud."

Lion, who was with the riding party, began to snarl, but did not leave Aramis, close to whom he was trotting along. Our friends had no swords, but each had his pistol. . . . Five or six vagabonds, dressed in tattered Confederate clothes, were seen trying to enter the stable, when the negro servants told them that there was not a horse in it,—and there was not, as Mr. Stannard had two to his carriage and Maud was riding the third.

"Well," said the leader of the gang, a villainous-looking rowdy, "the nigger is right; here come three horses. Hello! The devil take me if there ain't two Yanks with the lady. What can they be after here?"

Miss Maud had stopped, keeping Lion with her, while Aramis and Athos approached the gang.

"If they all have pistols," said Athos, "we shall have to shoot fast and straight, as there are five of them. We must not shoot to kill; corpses are inconvenient. Shoot the pistol hand; push them with your horse; knock them down, but if possible do not kill."

Within a few feet of the motley crowd Athos stopped and asked, "What are you doing on these premises? Leave at once, or we exterminate you."

"What?" said the one who had spoken before. "We do not answer questions put to us by blasted Yankees, and I command you to surrender or I shoot."

The words were scarcely out of his mouth before Athos and Aramis had made a sudden leap with their horses, falling in the very midst of the gang, knocking nearly every one off his feet and bruising them considerably. The leader had fired, as he said he would do, but the movement of Athos had been so sudden that the shot was harmless, and by that time Athos had turned around, pistol in hand, facing the fellow who had the pistol.

He was making ready to fire again when Athos, quick as lightning, fired in the hand, which Athos treated as he had done the right. There were only two pistols among the rascals, and Aramis took care of the fellow who had the second, charging on him full tilt as he was firing, the bullet scraping the horse's flank, making a skin wound, but the man was knocked senseless to the ground. Aramis had not even taken his pistol in hand. Two of the rascals were on the ground; the leader shot in both hands cried out, "Jump on the young devil and pull him off!"

Aramis went up to him, saying: "You jump, if you dare!"

Wounded in each hand, bleeding profusely, he jumped, but before he reached Aramis he had received a kick in the face from the latter's heel that spread him out. Those that were able were running off, but Athos stopped that and said: "Come back you rascals, or I shoot the last one of you!"

And back they came.

"I give you ten minutes to get out of here, and serve you notice that if ever you come back you will fare much worse than you have done today."

The one who Aramis ran against with his horse remained motionless until one of the negroes poured a bucket of water over him, when he revived.

"What is the use of wasting ammunition on such cattle?" asked Aramis.

By this time D'Artagnan was riding up. Taking in the situation at a glance, he told the fellows as they moved towards him to get out of the gate.

"Be quick and get out of here, or else I will take a hand in the play. You may thank your stars that I was late returning. Do not stop short of the mountains, or else woe unto you." Thus talking he escorted them to the gate.

He returned to his friends and to Miss Maud, who by this time had joined them. There was considerable blood on the ground, and Athos told a servant to clean it up.

"I hope, Miss Maud," said D'Artagnan as he saluted her, "that none of those fellows have insulted you, or upon my soul I'll go back and kill the last one of them."

"No," said she, laughing. "I do not believe they even saw me, surprised as they were by the sudden onslaught made by your friends, whom I thank with all my heart for the manner in which they have protected me. Gentlemen, I shall never forget it."

One of the negroes handed Athos two revolvers left on the ground by the outlaws, the only weapons they had; he was told to throw them in a pond nearby. The horses were stabled and the wound of Aramis's horse washed and stitched.

"Have you seen Walker coming back?"

"No," said Athos.

Miss Maud had retired, and D'Artagnan told his friends all about Walker; also what he had done when he met the Confederate colonel. They in return told D'Artagnan what Maud had told them about the negro servant who went to see his wife.

"We may go with him very soon. Well, my friends, this has been a fair day's work. I am inclined to think that I have scared Walker away, and you have punished those rascals so unmercifully that I do not think they will return here unless with friends to help them. Of course we shall be on the lookout. How have your horses behaved in the fray?"

"Excellently, they seem never to have done anything else in their lives but fight. They were surely trained for cavalry service, as they would not tramp upon the fellows when they were down on the ground."

"So much the better; I hate a skittish horse in time of action, and it is indeed lucky that none of those rascals were killed."

"Why?"

"Because if one of them had been, we would have had to explain before some judge how it all happened, while as it is, it is nobody's business, and we shall not be delayed. I have a mortal fear of delays at the present juncture."

It was late when dinner was served. Miss Maud received her guests in the dining room, her father having not returned. She felt happy in the company of three such gentlemenly and brave young men. . . . Mr. Stannard returned late; his trip had not been successful. Being told by his daughter what had happened during the afternoon, he thanked his guests for what they had done to protect his daughter and his house at the risk of their lives, and said that he would remain their debtor forever.

He told them that he had met General Ewell who told him that for the time being they were under marching orders, expecting to move at any moment, and consequently unable to comply with his request. Ewell looked for General Jackson at any time, and as soon as he arrived the army would move upon New Market, Strasburg, and

Winchester, up to the Potomac, hoping to capture Banks and his army, as the moment was propitious owing to the fact that General Banks's force had been much reduced to strengthen General McDowell.[1] If the march northward were postponed, which depended on the fighting near Richmond, he would with pleasure send a provost guard to the Stannard mansion.

He also told Mr. Stannard that a regiment of cavalry had that day been ordered to reconnoiter towards Luray, the Federal cavalry being near Columbia Bridge on the left bank of the Shenandoah. This was the regiment met by D'Artagnan in the morning.

All this was valuable information for our friends, and not a word of it was lost.

Mr. Stannard under the circumstances had decided to retire with his daughter to Richmond at the earliest possible moment, unless he could induce his guests to remain at the mansion. They informed him that much as they would desire to stay, it would be impossible for them to comply with his kind invitation, as they were compelled to move, probably on the very next day.

After parting with the Stannards that night, the friends had a conversation as to what they were to do. It was evident that Banks, with his ten thousand men would have to fall back before Jackson and his thirty thousand, the Federal lines being thus likely to get farther off. It was decided that they would that very night endeavor to secure John, the hostler, to show them the way [through the mountain gap to the Shenandoah].

John was given plenty of money for his trouble,—more than he had ever had in his life before,—and at once consented. He was told not to speak a word about it to any one.

"How long will it take us to get to the river?" asked D'Artagnan.

"Three hours, walking."

"Can we go by horseback?"

"Yes, but the gap is rocky and dark; it is easier to walk than ride when it is night. In daytime it can be done on horseback more easily."

"Well, we shall walk it. Make ready; we shall start at once as we must be back before daylight."

Within a quarter of an hour Aramis and D'Artagnan, with John to lead and Lion in the rear, were on their way. Athos was left at the mansion to defend the premises.[2]

CHAPTER 23

The Death of Walker

THERE WERE IN THE MOUNTAINS SEVERAL BANDS OF DESPERADOES, A murderous set. Among them were some brave men; most of them, however, were cowards. Young for the most part, they had enlisted in the Confederate army by the force of circumstances and surroundings, but had soon found out that they could not stand up before a manly foe, and they deserted. It was either to be shot by order of a court-martial or by the Yankees, and as they were not partial to Hobson's choice, they took to the woods and decided to do some shooting of their own.

Firearms were scarce among them and so was ammunition, but they all seemed to have the famous Bowie knife. The ranks of these men were increased with escaped convicts and others who had been obliged to seek refuge in the mountains to avoid punishment for their crimes. The leaders were, as a rule, escaped convicts who had commenced their vocation of land pirate before the war began.

Captain Alexander had told our friends in Richmond to beware of the scoundrels who infested the roads in the mountain districts which they were obliged to cross on their way southwest.

The atrocities committed by these villains were without number or parallel. Incendiarism, arson, rape, and murder, were pastimes for them. Outlaws of the worst kind, heartless and pitiless, they were only fit to be dealt with in the most summary manner, as the authorities had concluded to do: "Kill them on sight!". . .

The leader of the gang operating around Orange was one of those convicts, a rascal well known before the war under the name of Red Tom, because of his red hair.[1] He was a powerful man; he had at one time quite a little band under his command but had lost most of them, and himself included, there were only seven remaining.

They had a holy terror of the provost, and feared the Rebel soldiers even more than they did the Yankees. No men were ever taken prisoners by them,—to be shot like mad dogs was their fate. The only prisoners taken by the outlaws, and this was seldom, were women, who became the prey of their lust and whose fate was death, murdered in cold blood. It was horrible, and such a state of affairs was only made possible because of the exigencies of the war.

Tom and his gang were indeed a discomfited set after our friends had driven them from the Stannard mansion, two of their number being hurt considerably. Tom, whose face was very bloody and whose hands were mutilated and bleeding; the other, the one who had come in rough contact with Aramis's horse, whose legs as yet would hardly carry him. The wounds of Tom were washed off at the first pool and bandaged as well as possible. . . .

On reaching their camp they were met by two men of the gang, who were engaged in some other business while Tom and the rest had gone to the mansion; the gang had thought there was little to fear there, as there was only an old gentleman to oppose them. To be sure there were several negro servants on the premises, but the villains knew that they would not dare to lift a finger against a white man, no matter how great a rascal; in self-defense a negro might strike, perhaps, but never would take the offensive unless it was with murderous intent.

The whole gang had left that morning to take the remaining horses of Mr. Stannard, but on their way down to the road, before leaving the brush, they had detected a horseman working his way towards the west. It was John Walker, whom D'Artagnan had spoken with some five minutes before.

Walker was still thinking of the threat of the young Frenchman, and was in a brown study thinking over what he had better do, go to Conrad's store or back. He was very much perplexed over that warrant for perjury to be sworn by a respectable-looking man stopping at an elegant mansion of the neighborhood, and very slowly he moved westward before deciding what to do.

"Bob," said Tom, as they approached the road, "you stop that gentleman and see what he carries in his jeans; I will be ready to fire in case he shows fight."

And Bob arranged himself to meet Walker as near to Tom as possible, the fellows in the brush being entirely invisible.

Very politely he bade good morning to the rider, and quickly took hold of the reins with one hand and drew a large bowie from his belt, saying, "Old man, give us all your money and other valuables about you, or else here you die," and he brandished his weapon.

"All right," said Walker as cooly as he had spoken to D'Artagnan a short time before, and he put his hand in his pocket, but instead of a pocketbook it was a pistol that came out. Tom saw this from the brush, as he was not over twenty-five feet away, and having his pistol ready in his hand, he sent a bullet through the brain of the Virginian before the latter could fire. Bob almost at the same time gave him a blow with his knife.

Walker tumbled off his horse in the road, and Tim with his followers came near.

"Bob, take Bill with you and put this carcass in the gap and hide it there until we have time to dispose of it as we have disposed of others; tie the horse in the brush and in a few days we will trade him off. Here, boys, all of you help to put this gentleman on his horse, head one way, feet the other, and you can bet he never rode that way before."

It was done as ordered, and Tom with his four cutthroats directed their steps toward the mansion hardly three miles away, and we have seen what took place there.

Returning to the camp, our five rascals were hailed by Bob and Bill.

"What in the name of the devil is the matter with you all? You look like a funeral procession; you have been robbed instead of the other fellow?"

"Shut up," growled Tom. "We have been licked, well licked; that is all, and it is the first time, too. Where is the carcass you brought here?"

"In the gap."

"How much money?"

"Over three hundred dollars and a gold watch. He might have been alive now, riding his plug, had he quietly given up his swag."

"Yes, and you would be a dead man now, if I had not killed him." . . .

CHAPTER 24

The Gap

JOHN PROVIDED HIMSELF WITH THE LANTERN WHICH HE USUALLY CARRIED on his trips, as it was indispensable in the passage of the gap during the night, for it was darkness itself between the granite walls.

A gap is a cleft in a mountain from top to bottom and from one end to the other. The width is not uniform, but as a rule is very narrow, and nearly all of them are impracticable for highway purposes. Man on foot, and even horseback, can get through. It is, however, always dangerous, as some bit of rock may come tumbling down any time from hundreds of feet high. This mountain, which is a part of the Blue Ridge, is some three hundred feet high where the gap is entered, and almost perpendicular. It is seldom less in height and at places it reaches one thousand feet.

On his trip from the Stannard mansion to the Columbian Furnace, by going through the gap, John saved some five miles of walking and climbing as against the regular road leading between the two places. Within the gap it is damp and dreary, in places wet; light is almost invisible, even during the day; at night the stars are hardly visible from the bottom.[1] These gaps,—there are several of them it is said,—may be called the beds of creeks permitting the overflow of waters on the east side to rush through to the Shenandoah, and at times these places become very dangerous.

John led the way, D'Artagnan came next, then Aramis and Lion, who seldom parted from the latter. They were obliged to travel in Indian file, the path in the brush and timber being invisible except to the practiced eye of John, who was one of the few darkies master of all the intricacies of this route.

Nearing the gap, within a few steps of it, Lion howled as dogs usually do when death is around, and Aramis had to silence him as it made a tremendous noise so near the granite walls of the mountain. At the entrance of the gap the party stopped to enable John to light his lantern but Lion dashed on ahead, and being within the gap some fifteen or twenty steps, he again gave a plaintive howl.

"Strange," said John, "there must be someone dead in there."

Lifting the lantern they proceeded on their way, and very soon John reached Lion; lowering his lantern he exclaimed: "Why, here is a dead man!"

Lion, true to his natural instincts of hunting bodies in the snows of St. Bernard, had his paw upon the breast of the corpse and howled his plaintive and mournful cry. He was again silenced, and the party approached to look at the body.

"Why," exclaimed D'Artagnan, "upon my soul, it is the body of John Walker with a bullet in his brain! What an extraordinary occurrence to find him dead. It is a job that we shall not have to do. But how has his corpse come here, and where is his horse?"

"Probably the men who came to the mansion, the fellows you drove away, met him on the road and killed him."

"John, see if there is anything left in his pockets."

He looked and found nothing; in fact all the pockets were turned inside out.

"He has been murdered and robbed," said John. "His body was brought here on his horse, and hidden in the gap where no person was likely to find him for a long time, and the horse was then taken to the rascals' camp until they can sell it."

"That must be it. But let us pull his body out of the gap and drag it in the bush. It might scare our horses in case we come this way. I do not fancy the idea of my horse prancing around here, knocking my shoulders and legs against those boulder walls."

They proceeded to do as suggested by D'Artagnan, and John Walker was soon disposed of.

The two friends always spoke French except when addressing John.

"Aramis, I take this as a good omen. The killing of this villain by some other hands than ours removes him from our path just at the time when we are to cross the lines; it must mean good luck."

"So it may be! He has been the bitterest enemy we had, even to the very hour of his death."

"Do not doubt it. I am glad we did not kill any of those rascals this morning; they have done us a good turn."

The corpse once removed, they went their way through the gap after John notified them not to look above their heads but to look all the time straight before them, and follow in his footsteps. John told them this, as he said, because they might fall down in their tracks in case they did look up. The distance seems so great from the bottom of the gap to the almost imperceptible opening above that it would make one dizzy at once, so dizzy that they would fall, as John himself had. He therefore gave them timely notice, which, however, was not scrupulously followed until both of them had met the same experience.

"Why," said D'Artagnan, picking himself up, "if we find out nothing else tonight than the death of John Walker, it will be a most satisfactory tramp that we are taking now, disagreeable as it is.

"Yes, indeed, but do try to keep on your feet." . . .

"So far as we have gone on this road," said Aramis, "I do not see why we could not have come horseback. The walking is not good, but our horses have a much surer footing then we have."

"That is true, but John thought it better for us to walk it this time, and he is a very sensible man."

They reached the western end of the gap in good time. They stepped out of it all of a sudden just as they had entered it, the mountain being almost perpendicular at both sides. Within the walls the atmosphere was murky and sticky, but as soon as they reached the outside it was very balmy. John extinguished his light at once for fear that it might immediately become a target for some picket guards.

They were now on the bottom extending along the right bank of the Shenandoah, some two miles in width at that place, the soil of which is very productive, and splendid ferns covered the whole valley. Just now, however, it was very much deserted on account of the warmth, and John knew his way, dark as it was. It must have been near midnight. It was much clearer than within the gap, the sky being full of stars.

John was sure of his way. It seemed that the line he had followed from the time they had left the mansion was a perfect beeline, as it nearly was. The guide made his path to the gap, and once out of the gap he made a straight line to the river, making a nine miles' walk when by the road it was fully fifteen. . . .

Having reached the river, John said, "Here we are, gentlemen; do you mean to cross?

"No, but how do you cross?"

"Most of the time I swim it; sometimes my wife waits for me right here with a little boat."

"Can horses cross the river here?"

"Yes, but they will have to swim some fifty yards in a rather swift current. The next bridge below is called Columbia Bridge; I heard yesterday that the Yankees had burned it."

Lion went to the river and cooled himself by lying in the water.

"If this dog could come with us when we leave, he would pilot us right straight to this place. I confess it would puzzle me to find this place in a dark night like this."

"Yes, it would surely be a difficult task, for I see nothing at all here to attract one's attention."

"John, is there anything by which you guide yourself to reach this spot as you travel this path?"

"There used to be a high smokestack on the other side at the Columbian Furnace. Day and night the work was going on, and the sparks coming out with the smoke now and then were my guide at the start, but the stack has fallen down lately, and the works have been destroyed. I have followed this path so many times that I could almost go it blindfolded."

John also told them that Saturday last, when he came here to see his wife, the Yankees had their cavalry pickets on the ridge just north of the Furnace, some three miles away, while the Rebels had theirs near the Furnace.

"How strong was the Rebel picket?" asked D'Artagnan.

"Some twelve men."

As to the road, he told them that the road near the river on the other side led straight to New Market, where the Federal headquarters were located.

"Aramis, this is the place where we are going to cross and enter the Federal lines within a short time. Once across the river, there may be some danger but we cannot expect to get through in a coach-and-four."

They had been sitting close to the bank on the river, resting and smoking cigars, with Lion near them. But suddenly he had risen on all fours, head erect, sniffing down the river.

"Somebody is coming," said Aramis. "Be quiet, Lion!"

"It is someone on the pike about fifty steps away," said John, "on the road from Luray to Conrad's Store. Lion will not bark, and whoever it is will go by without knowing that we are here."

Lion remained with his head erect, on guard against sudden surprise, and as John said, did not bark. The noise became more dense and compact; very soon the clinking of sabres against horses' flanks and the spurs of riders indicated that it was a body of cavalry moving up the valley.

"It is doubtless the regiment that left Conrad this morning in reconnaissance when I was there, and is now returning to its camp. I think we are all right here. When they have gone by we shall go back. Aramis, we'll cross this river tonight."

"Thank the Lord for that!"

Patting Lion on the head, Aramis added, "Good Lion, we shall soon have to part company, my boy. What can possibly have caused this beautiful beast to take such a sudden attachment to me? It will certainly pain me to part with him."

The dog, seeming to understand, rubbed his big head against Aramis as if in sorrow.

John was fast asleep on the ground. It took about a quarter of an hour for the regiment to pass, showing by its straggling along that it had a hard day's work. John was roused, and they made their way back as they had come.

"John, before you come to the pike take a sharp look around; we want no trouble with the cavalrymen."

As John could see nothing and Lion made no sign of alarm, they crossed the pike and went direct to the gap. At four o'clock they reached the mansion and John was told to keep himself in readiness for another trip the coming night, and was enjoined to keep silence.

Athos was most anxious to hear the news, but when he went to his friends' rooms at six o'clock he had to shake them before they wakened. It had been a hard night's work, and they were not used to such rough exercise.

"It is the first and last time," said Aramis, "that I will undertake such an abominable trip on foot, I assure you."

"That's all right; we shall go horseback next time now that we know how to go."

"When shall we start?" asked Athos.

"Today," said D'Artagnan.

He was told all about the trip, and expressed his satisfaction when he was informed about the death of Walker, which by his friends as by himself was accepted as the work of the rascals whom they had driven from the Stannard mansion; there could be no other explanation. The fact that he was dead and gone was all they cared about.

At breakfast D'Artagnan informed Mr. Stannard that it had become necessary for them to leave during the day, and thanked him and his daughter for the kind manner in which they had been treated.

For heaven's sake do not mention it," said the old gentleman, "we can never repay you for what you have done for us yesterday. Maud, you will make arrangements to leave for Richmond tomorrow; we shall proceed without delay." . . .

"Father, ever since those gentlemen have arrived I have noticed that Lion has taken a great fancy for one of them, in fact he has entirely deserted me and will be of no use whatever in Richmond. Will you allow me to dispose of him?"

"He is yours, and you can do with him what you please."

Addressing Aramis, she said, "He seems to have selected you for master, sir, and my friend Alice who knows him well will be happy to learn that he is yours. Of course I cannot, and will never, I fear, be able to sufficiently acknowledge the debt of gratitude I owe you and your friend for having stood between me and danger, when, at the risk of your lives you drove those men away yesterday. I shall never forget it, and regret exceedingly that we must part after so short an acquaintance."

"Miss Maud, I know not what to say. If you had asked me, 'What do you desire?' I would have said, 'Give me Lion!' But probably I would not have dared to do so.

"I presume you know that ultimately I intend to return to Richmond; I shall then have the honor and the pleasure of meeting you again. But what Athos and myself did for you yesterday any two gentlemen would have done, and we deserve no thanks for doing our duty. We rejoice that the occasion may remind you of us, especially myself, for I am jealous of the good opinion of so dear a friend of Miss Alice as you are. As a personal favor, may I ask you to hand her a letter?"

"Miss Maud," said Athos, "our friend would like to say more, but he really cannot say it all. I assure you that I also am jealous of your good opinion,—for your own sake first, and for that of Miss Alice next. This war will not last forever, and the time will come when I also shall return, and I pray that I may meet you then."

"Mr. Stannard," said D'Artagnan with a broad and kind smile, "it seems to me that my friends are making arrangements for the future from which I am excluded. I don't know that I shall ever return, but I beg to assure you, sir, and you, Miss, that I shall ever be your most humble servant."

Athos and Miss Maud had been together a good portion of the previous evening, while his friends were reconnoitering the road over which they meant to make a dash for liberty, long after the old gentleman had retired. The natural inclination which from the start had attracted one toward the other had not been diminished,—on the contrary, and there is no telling what a few days more would have revealed, or what Athos would have seen fit to promise and she to accept.

CHAPTER 25

Alice Arrived

ABOUT ONE O'CLOCK OF THE AFTERNOON, A CONFEDERATE AMBULANCE drawn by four mules stopped in front of the mansion. Miss Maud and Athos were on the portico at the time, Aramis and D'Artagnan having gone to the stable to see John and give him final instructions.

A lady whom Miss Maude at once recognized as Alice alighted from the ambulance and she rushed to meet her with a sweet embrace. Alice, seeing Athos, asked quickly, "Where are the others?"

"Oh, they are not far; do not fret, darling; they are all here, but they leave today."

The attendant with the ambulance asked Alice whether she had done with the ambulance, and she told him that she had, and that he could return.

"Miss Alice," said Athos, "allow me to greet you with the assurance that I am happy to see you. Please excuse me for a few minutes; I will look up my friends and inform them of your arrival."

"How is it that they are still here, dear Maud? I thought that he was gone, but yet I feel happy at the thought of seeing him once again."

"They leave this afternoon, and I am sorry that they are going."

"They must leave, Maud, the sooner the better. I feel there is danger for them in remaining. I will tell you all about it when I have time. All are perfect gentlemen, but they sympathize with the North. They came for a great and heroic purpose; they failed, and they must depart. Help me, Maud, to save them!"

"I will do all I can to please you, darling. I feel a strange interest in one of them."

"How strange?" asked Alice with a smile.

"You are too inquisitive. I will tell you when I have time," and she placed her hand over Alice's mouth as though to close it. "I wrote you yesterday; my letter will reach your home today. In it I told you that the two called Athos and Aramis,—strange names, are they not?—probably saved my life yesterday. The two fought against five villains and drove them away in a most dashing manner. You love Aramis dearly, Alice?"

"Can you blame me? I would die several deaths to save his life. I told him that you were such a charming girl,—not to stay here too long."

Maud did not allow her to finish.

"You naughty Alice, stop at once! Short of the attention that a gentlemen is obliged to give a lady, whether he desires it or not, I really do not believe he could tell you the color of my hair, surely not that of my eyes. Athos, on the contrary, has been very attentive, and I think could tell you the color of both hair and eyes. Now you are happy, are you not? We will not quarrel over them. All three are perfect, it seems to me, but I prefer the one you have just seen."

"Maud, they must get across the lines immediately."

"The lines are only a few miles from here, and judging from what Mr. Athos told me last evening,—we were together and alone for at least two hours, so you see there is no reason to be jealous, for they were exceedingly delicious hours,—I am inclined to think that the road was reconnoitered last night, and that they will start today."

"I have not seen your father. Where is he?"

"We leave for Richmond tomorrow, and he has gone to make preparations for the trip."

"Why to hateful Richmond, where men and women are breathing nothing but hate and war?"

"I know, but we are exposed to great dangers here, and Father is uneasy for me, as he is all alone to protect me and he is becoming too feeble to offer much resistance."

"Well, then we shall go together tomorrow, and you will stop with me, if I go back at all."

"What do you mean by saying, 'if I go back at all?'"

Athos and his friends appeared at the door of the parlor.

"Enter, gentlemen," said Maud. Alice at once rushed to Aramis, and placing her hands on his shoulders, not daring in the presence of others to be more demonstrative, looked him in the eyes and said: "I was in hopes that you had gone and were safe among your people, and yet I am so happy to see you." Then recognizing Athos and D'Artagnan she added, "And you also, gentlemen."

Aramis took Alice's arm, then said to her friend: "Miss Maud, I had not the least idea that this moment of great happiness was reserved for me this day. I beg to thank her for having made it possible. My only regret is that I am obliged to leave without her."

"Can you not take me with you?" Alice asked.

Maud went near her friend.

"Miss Alice," said Aramis, "God is my witness that if it were possible you would come along. I would even take Miss Maud to keep you company, but it is impossible. We will risk our lives, but I would not risk your lives for the world."

"Yes, I thought it was impossible," said Alice. "And now listen and remember what I tell you. I left Richmond this morning, and on the train was General Jackson. My father was along, he was ordered to go with the general yesterday to attend to some ordnance business at Fort Republic, and I asked him to let me go with him to visit you, dear Maud. The general telegraphed ahead to have an ambulance ready for me at Gordonsville to bring me here.

"The general commences his march, so I heard him say, tomorrow morning, and intends to go to Harpers Ferry on the Potomac by way of New Market, Strasburg, and Winchester, and may cross and go to Washington in case Lee defeats McClellan. He will have 30,000 men with him, and he means to march rapidly; General Ewell will be in the lead."

"Thank you, Miss Alice, for this information," said D'Artagnan. "We shall reach our lines sometime during the coming night, and the moment for departing is propitious. Knowing now, Miss Maud, that we are against the South, I trust that we will not lose any of your good opinion, if we have been so fortunate as to have won it. Men cannot all agree, no matter how good those men."

"Aramis is a great winner by our visit to Richmond," continued D'Artagnan. "What of Athos?—I do not know, but he also may be a winner. I am the only loser; I have not won a heart, and probably will not, for the time is short,—we leave at six."

The party broke up. Alice went her way with Aramis and Lion; Athos his, with Maud; and D'Artagnan, his, to the stable, where he fixed the ammunition to keep it safe while crossing the river. The parting meal was sad in the extreme. D'Artagnan did wonders to make it more cheerful, but it was labor lost. The question with the ladies was "How will we know when you are safe?"

"Miss Maud," said D'Artagnan, "Lend us John for a few hours and he will, on his return, tell you all about it."

The time for leaving had come. D'Artagnan was on horseback already, and his adieus were those of a friend. It took more time for Aramis and Athos. He gave them time, and finally startled them by crying in his stentorian voice "Time!" Maud and Alice remained together alone. Our Frenchmen were gone, with John in the lead on foot. In Indian file with Lion in the rear, they followed the same road they had taken the night before.[1]

"Now boys," said D'Artagnan, "I smell a fight. See that your pistols and ammunition are all right. I have prepared a little package for each of you that you will tie on your heads with a handkerchief, with your hats over it, before we cross the river. The pistols you will hang around your necks, the swords will take care of themselves.

"I had John try the horses to see if they could swim; he used the great pond in the park. Of course all horses swim, but it is hard to get some in the water. Ours went right in, and they behaved like ducks. As to our passes, they must not be found upon us on the other side of the river, so you had better wrap them around a bullet previous to our entering the Shenandoah and sink them in the river before we get out."

Athos and Aramis had caught the instructions, and in the hope of a fight their spirits revived.

CHAPTER 26

Crossing the Shenandoah

DURING 1862 THE VALLEY OF THE SHENANDOAH BECAME OF THE greatest military importance, and its possession was being tenaciously contested by both Federals and Confederates. It was the geographical artery leading from the South towards Washington, and from the North towards the South; then too, it was yet rich in grain and stock, with countless meadows in prime condition for the support of both Confederate and Federal cavalry, thus enabling them to move very rapidly. But in the early spring of that year the Valley had become even more important than before, as General McClellan had changed his front and was advancing upon Richmond by the way of Yorktown on the [Virginia] Peninsula. His base was near Fortress Monroe instead of near Washington, thus offering to the Confederates the opportunity to turn the Federal right, as also to make raids against Washington.

Summing up the several years' fighting in the valley, two great central figures predominate all the rest: T. J. "Stonewall" Jackson on one side and P. H. "Little Phil" Sheridan on the other. Their names will live among the legendaries which will be transmitted from generation to generation as those of American heroes. Many others distinguished themselves and won laurels, but those two overshadow all the rest.

General Jackson commenced the fighting in March 1862 and impressed his name upon the history of the Valley from Harpers Ferry to Harrisonburg in a manner that never will be forgotten, while General Sheridan carved his upon the granite of the Allegheny Mountains, when in the fall of 1864, he rushed and crushed back the victorious legions of

Jubal Early, riding that famous twenty miles from Winchester to the bat-tlefield of Cedar Creek, plucking victory from the midst of a general rout.[1] After nearly three years of hard fighting the Valley was in Federal hands; the last gun had been fired there.

It is probable that the Valley might have been won in 1862 and many lives saved, had a soldier been in command of [Federal] forces there when Jackson made his first dash in Winchester during the month of March of that year; but [General] Banks was not a soldier. Yet one year later, in the face of his failure in the Shenandoah, Banks was given a still more impor-tant command in the Red River Valley; he was again beaten, his army dri-ven back to the Mississippi. General Shields, one of Banks's division commanders on the Shenandoah, whipped Jackson in March 1862; he was a soldier. And General A. J. Smith, one of Banks's division comman-ders in the Red River campaign, whipped the Confederates every time he came in contact with them; he also was a soldier. Banks was only a fight-ing lawyer and a politician. Politics can be a bane in time of war as well as in time of peace, and political appointments in the army have cost Amer-ica thousands of her very bravest and most promising sons. . . .

But it was now about the middle of May [1862], and the day had arrived when our three friends had decided to cross the Confederate lines; they were going to burn their bridges behind them. They must succeed in reaching the Federal lines or die in the attempt.

They had left the Stannard mansion as we have seen and had reached the western side of the gap before it was dark enough to venture horse-back upon the bottom which they had to cross before reaching the river. They dismounted, leaving John in charge of their horses, and stepping outside they took a look over the ground they had to cross and the lay of the mountain on the other side of the river. No fires could be distin-guished anywhere indicative of camp or bivouac.

"The crossing of that river," said D'Artagnan, "is a small affair, but the manner of crossing is an important proposition."

"What do you mean?"

"I mean,—shall we all three get out at the same point on the other side, or shall we strike three different places? It is possible that Rebel pick-ets may be somewhere about the point we strike, or within hearing dis-tance of it. In that case we shall receive a volley from their rifles, fired at random, it is true, as they will only hear the horses splashing in the water. So we ought to make as little noise as possible, and one horse makes less noise than three."

"Why not send John ahead to find out? Swimming over, he will not make any noise."

"That strikes me favorably, but is it not somewhat risky? I have the utmost confidence in the man, yet there is no telling what he might do if he found himself in a tight box. I would go myself if I were a first-class swimmer, but I am not."

"I am," said Aramis, "and I warrant you nobody will hear me. I can swim or float right by a picket without being noticed at all."

"Very well, you are the man. Lion is sure to follow you, and he will give you the benefit of his scenting power. Enough for the present. It is dark now; let us proceed and we shall decide on our future movements when you have taken a look at the other side."

They mounted their horses and, following John, moved towards the river, which they soon reached.

"Now Aramis, off with you. Once on the other side examine the surroundings for at least one mile so that we may have an idea of the situation over there."

"Say, John, how is the water on the other side? Is it deep enough for one to lie on his back and float down?" asked Aramis.

"The deepest part of the river is about the middle, and it remains deep until within a few yards of the other side."

Without further ado Aramis stripped and went in, with Lion in his wake.

"B–r–r–ah," he was heard to exclaim, and then said, "This water is very cold."

"Yes," said John to the others, "it is early in the season yet and the mountain springs are very cold, but the chill will soon be taken out of him after he begins to swim."

Athos struck a match, and looking at his watch said, "Ten o'clock."

"Gentlemen," said John, "it will take your friend at least an hour to make the trip."

John was told by D'Artagnan to go near the pike so as to advise them if anything took place there to cause alarm, and the two friends remained together by the water's edge, one of them holding Aramis's horse.

Here they were for the first time in six weeks really separated; one of the three had gone. He was out of reach, swimming away entirely invisible because of the darkness. In case of accident his friends were unable to assist him.

"Athos, I feel all out of sorts with Aramis gone in that water; how long is he gone?"

"Not over a quarter of an hour."

"It seems to me much longer. Should we not fix a place so that we may make a light to show him where to land on his return?"

"I hardly think it necessary; the light might be noticed by others on the opposite side. Lion is sure to find his way back here."

"To be sure. I had forgotten all about the dog in my anxiety for Aramis."

The night was very dark, as few stars could be seen; the clouds were fleeting fast, and nothing was to be heard save occasional chafing at the bits by the horses, and the rippling of the water in its current down the river on the way towards the Potomac and Washington, the goal of their hopes.

"Athos, I have not been as nervous since we started on this trip. It seems to me that I have forgotten something and cannot think what it is; the time seems so awfully long, only half an hour since our friend started."

"You have no fears for Aramis, have you?"

"I do not know,—yes, and no. There is no telling what may happen, and we are not near to help him. In case anything does, he has no weapon to defend himself. Perhaps I was wrong; we should have gone together, yet I thought it was for the best, as we need to be exceedingly prudent. Hark! Do you hear anything?"

"Yes, the sound of bugles far away up the river; they are hardly audible. It may be taps."

"It must be so. Possibly the regiment of cavalry I visited yesterday morning some six miles away. Nearly all the horses were black, and they must belong to General Ashby's Black Horse.[2] I heard he was a most skillful, daring, and dashing leader who made himself once again famous some two months since, when he covered Stonewall Jackson's retreat from Winchester pursued by General Shields's advance, giving him no rest until he was driven far away south. After his victory Shields was ordered to fall back on Strasburg some fifty miles north. That is what Banks calls generalship. What time is it now, Athos?"

"Yet a quarter of an hour to wait; but it may take longer than anticipated, as Aramis will do his work thoroughly."

"No shooting has yet taken place on the other side, or we would surely have heard it, and I begin to breathe more freely. What is the matter with the horses? They are pricking up their ears, looking at the river; they can hear and see better than we can."

D'Artagnan dismounted, and lying flat on the sand near the water, called out in subdued tones: "Is it you, Aramis?"

The answer soon came back: "Yes!"

"I never was so happy in my life," said D'Artagnan as he arose. "Really I was not born to be a soldier."

"If you were not, I would like to know the one who was."

"I have been trembling and shaking for nearly an hour as if I had a chill."

Lion was the first to land at the very spot where D'Artagnan stood, and was greeted with a friendly patting on the head. Very soon afterward came Aramis, who was at once clasped his friend's arms, as though they had been separated for years. . . .

"My!" exclaimed Aramis. "How cold that water, and how balmy it feels here. Do you know that if it had not been for Lion it would have taken me a long time to find this spot? Crossing the river on my way over I drifted somewhat with the current; not much, I assure you, for I worked as hard as I could to warm myself up to keep from cramping. Coming back I had to swim against the current, and it made me lose my bearings. I then told Lion: 'Go!' He took the lead and brought me right back to you. I assure you that I felt lonesome all by myself."

"Do not mention it," said D'Artagnan, "I never was so restless in my life."

Aramis soon jumped into his clothes and said: "Miss Maud Stannard has given me a real treasure; Lion is the most intelligent dog I have ever seen; he seemed to know what I went over for. On the other side of this river the water does not reach the bank as it does here; there is some sort of sandy beach between the water and the bank, a regular slope on which horses can walk. The mountain is very near the bank of the river, and between the two, there is a turnpike over which I labored hard with my bare feet."

"I followed the beach on my way down for nearly a mile, and came back by the road," continued Aramis. "I did not see a soul, heard nothing but a bugle call far away up the river, just at the time I reached the beach. Lion struck no trail at all; he remained perfectly calm, only raising his head now and then, sniffing as if to get the scent of some suspicious object. There is nothing over there to disturb our landing within my sphere of observation."

"By the way, did you recognize the bugle call? We heard it, but it was too faint; we could not make it out."

"I heard it fairly well, as the current of the water strikes the other side, and I took it to be 'Boots and Saddles.' However, I am not well enough acquainted with cavalry calls to be sure of it. If I am not mistaken in the call, we have no time to lose, as we were told by Miss Alice that General Jackson was coming this way."

"It does not matter what call it was, after all, since we are in the saddle and on the move," said D'Artagnan. "From Aramis's description of the other side we shall follow that sand beach as far as we can; it will be next to impossible to hear us move on it.

"I will land first, then you, Athos, some distance below, and then Aramis. Having halted some few minutes, I will move towards Athos, and together we shall move towards Aramis. Let us not mistake gun shot or army revolver shot for our own pistol shots; they are easily distinguished. We must rally at once when one of us fires, so that we may assist one another."

John came to them from the pike and said: "Gentlemen, I hear the same noise we heard last night when the cavalry came this way. It is a good piece away yet, I judge, and I am sure some heavy wagons are along, as I hear the rumbling noise of wheels. It comes from the direction of Conrad's Store."

"How long will it be, do you think, before they reach here?"

"Some twenty minutes or so, I dare say."

"This cavalry is bound for Luray once again. The rumbling noise that John speaks of must be artillery, and General Banks will soon know it," said D'Artagnan.

"Tell the ladies," said Aramis to John, "that you have seen us cross the river; that the other side, so far as personal observation shows, is all right, and that we expect to be within the Federal lines by daylight. Also tell Miss Alice that I will communicate with her as agreed, when I reach Washington."

"Yes, sir."

"And if you hear any shooting on the other side, you must not mention it to the ladies, as it would alarm them."

"I will not, sir. Gentlemen, may God bless you," and he kissed the hand of each one. He then hugged Lion's neck and kissed him on the head. The poor fellow had been the dog's keeper ever since it was a pup, and was much attached to him. John's voice was broken with sobs when he told them as a final bit of advice: "I forgot to tell you that when you have traveled some six miles down the river you will reach a little creek. The road crosses it some fifty yards below the ruins of the old Furnace works, where the Rebel pickets are usually posted. The creek must be dry now. If you could follow the sandy beach on the other side all the way down past the creek you would, I think, miss the pickets altogether until you reach the Federal outposts."

"Thanks, John. Now, my good man, cross the pike quickly so that you may not be caught by the cavalry. Good-bye."

"Now," said D'Artagnan to his friends, "here comes the rub; we burn our bridges behind us. And remember, we live or die together, as we must not be taken prisoners a second time."

Indeed, this was the time that made these brave souls somewhat mindful of the immediate future, as within four or five hours they must be in General Banks's lines, or in all probability dead. They were not men to hesitate as to their line of action now, and death never had any great terror for them. But here they were, at the very point of slipping through the Rebel lines, the sole object they had in view of late, and which they were now proceeding to perform. They were ready to fight the pickets, if necessary, but were not desirous to do so; the uncertainty of their location and their numbers, were matters of importance they yet knew nothing about.

Old soldiers well remember the anxiety in their ranks while approaching a hidden force of the foe just previous to the attack; our friends were not only in the same condition but even more so, for there were only three of them and retreat was out of the question. It was as D'Artagnan had said,—"Live or die together!" The moment was indeed solemn for them.

"Have you got your ammunition and pistols secured? Are your passes ready to be thrown into the river? They have ceased to be safeguards; they would cost us our heads now. We shall part company, each one of us to go as is understood when we reach deep water."

"We are ready."

"Well, here goes!" and they all three entered the river with Lion behind them.

John, after waiting sometime near the gap to hear if any shooting took place, moved sadly and slowly on his way back to the Stannard mansion. He had heard no shooting before entering the gap, within it he could not possibly have heard any. He reached the mansion about daylight, and he said to himself: "They are with their friends now, or they are dead."

Alice and Maud were waiting for John's return, having found it impossible to retire. They remained together in the parlor, sad and lonely, until John arrived at about five o'clock. He delivered Aramis's message and added that the gentlemen crossed the river successfully and that for the next hour he heard no shooting at all, and that therefore they must have been successful in eluding the vigilance of the Confederate pickets.

"Thank God!" said Alice.

A few hours later Mr. Stannard and the two young ladies were on their way to Richmond, while those who gave them so much concern had just succeeded in reaching the road that led to Washington.

CHAPTER 27

Under the Old Flag

IT TOOK ABOUT THREE-QUARTERS OF AN HOUR FOR THE THREE TO MEET on the other side of the river at the place where Aramis had landed a short time before, and where he was awaiting near the water's edge the arrival of his two friends. Each had crossed the river as agreed, and as well as he could; but it was not without difficulty, as the current was swift, the bottom irregular, with now and then large rocks projecting a few feet above the surface of the water. It must have been about twelve o'clock when they met.

"Has Lion taken the scent of anything since you landed?" asked D'Artagnan of Aramis.

"He has not. At least he has not barked, nor snarled. It is so dark I am unable to watch him."

Aramis was holding his horse, as he had been obliged to dismount to take his boots off to let the water run out, and had not yet mounted as he was waiting for his friends.

"But my, how dark it is here," [said D'Artagnan,] "surely darker than it was on the other side. It must be on account of that mountain at the very foot of which we are. We will dismount like Aramis and lead the horses. Within one hour and a half we ought to reach the creek that John spoke of."

"A good idea," said Athos. "We are soaking wet to the armpits, and the walking will warm us up."

They kept as near the water as possible, feeling assured that no one could see them from the pike nor hear them as they walked upon the sand. On the contrary they could hear any one moving on the pike. If the moon had shone it would have been different; the water's radiancy would have shown their shadows plainly from the pike.

After walking about half an hour they felt warm enough to mount their horses again. It was about half-past one when they found that the sand beach was narrowing to a point, and they concluded that the creek running by the Furnace must be near. They at once resolved to take the pike and run the gauntlet, if gauntlet there were, relying solely upon the keen eyesight of their horses to keep the main road.

"The pickets are probably on this side of the creek, and it seems to me that Lion ought to catch their scent, if they are. Are you sure the dog is here?"

"He walks by my side," said Aramis. "Before we mounted I could now and then feel him. Be sure of one thing, he will not leave us."

"Let us cross the creek. If we are ordered to halt, we shall at once put our horses on the run. Surely we cannot be seen; they will have to fire by the sound, and the faster we go the less chance of being hit."

They rode along the pike a short while and soon found themselves going downhill; it was the creek. The noise of their horses' hoofs upon the pike was perfectly audible in the silence of the night.

While ascending the hill on the other side of the creek, the command "Halt, who comes there!" rang out clear and strong. It was not over fifty feet away on the left, and they at once put their horses at full speed. Two shots were fired immediately, but without effect; two more were fired soon afterwards; this time the whiz of bullets was heard. They flew over the pike for a mile or two. No more shots were fired, and they stopped to find out if they were pursued; nothing could be heard. They had run the gauntlet successfully.

"Thank God!" exclaimed D'Artagnan. "We are safe! John was mistaken; their pickets were on this side of the creek. Ours cannot be far off, that is sure, and we had better wait here until daylight has set in; there is no need to be shot at again."

"Strange they have not given us the chase."

"It proves that our pickets are near, or else they would have done so."

The firing had been heard by the Federal outpost; only four shots, it is true, but it put them on their guard. Daylight came at last. It had been a long night for our friends, one full of excitement, uncertainty, and danger. They felt free now. They found themselves on the top of a plateau, on a pike with old-fashioned rail fences on either side. Lion was taking a much-needed rest, spread out full length on the grass by the road.

"Now let us move. We will in all probability be halted again, but by our men this time."

They rode some three miles and then perceived a Federal cavalry outpost in the land. They at once shook their hats way above their heads in sign of joy, but were sternly greeted with the command "Halt, who comes there!" It came ringing into their ears as the very sweetest music; it was answered by the word "Friends!"

They dismounted and threw their hats up in the most hilarious way and cheered for Abraham Lincoln. A half-dozen cavalrymen with carbines on the advance, ready for business, marched upon them.

"Who are you, and where do you come from?"

"Late officers of the 53rd New York Volunteers; escaped prisoners from Richmond," said D'Artagnan. "General Banks knows us well; so does Captain Crosby of his staff. We would like to see the general as soon as possible, as we have most important news to communicate to him."

This outpost belonged to an Indiana cavalry regiment, and they were at once taken to the headquarters, some two miles away, of [Major George Henry] Chapman. He was told that General Jackson had started from Fort Republic that morning early, if not during the night, on his way to New Market and Strasburg.[1]

Upon their request they were sent under escort to General Banks, who had passed the night at New Market. It was about eight o'clock when they reached headquarters, a brick house on the west side of the road, and they found the general in the yard ready to mount his horse. They approached him and he at once recognized them.

"Hello, where do you come from, young men? We at Washington were at a loss to know what had become of you."

D'Artagnan told him in a few words what they had been at, and how they got the information about General Jackson's advance with a large force for the purpose of attacking him at once.

"This information is correct?"

"Yes, General; we have it from a lady who heard Jackson himself say so yesterday morning. While we were on the point of crossing the Shenandoah last night, a cavalry force was moving down the river towards Luray on the other side of the river. I am in a position to know that a cavalry regiment went in that direction the day before yesterday from Conrad's Store, returning late that night."

"Yes, I know. We saw them and were ready for them as we thought they might attempt to cross the river, but they found the bridge destroyed. We failed to see them yesterday."

"Well, that same force must now be at, or near, Luray again."

This information was at once sent to Colonel Wyndham, U.S.A., in charge of the cavalry at the time,[2] who took the necessary measures to delay the advance of General Jackson as much as possible, while orders were given by General Banks for the infantry and the trains to immediately fall back upon Strasburg by the way of Woodstock, as his force was too small to resist Jackson. The army of General Banks had been reduced about one-half, General Shields's division having received orders from the War Department to move to Front Royal, preparatory to joining General McDowell at Fredericksburg, thence to move towards Richmond to assist General McClellan. Shields was yet at Front Royal, some fifteen miles from Strasburg.

"General," said D'Artagnan, "we will remain with you today if you allow us. When you reach Strasburg we will beg your leave to return to Washington."

"All right, you can join my staff. By the way, I secured a captaincy for you on the staff of General Grover, who will soon sail towards New Orleans, where he will be in need of an officer speaking French on his staff. It was a few days after you left, but I could not find you; I suppose the appointment may have lapsed. See about this as soon as you arrive in Washington."[3]

"How long before you will leave here?"

"I will go and take a look toward Columbia Furnace within one hour."

Our friends were in great glee; their happiness had no bounds. They had forgotten all about breakfast for themselves and feed for their horses. They took immediate steps to supply themselves with the necessary, and within an hour were again horseback by the side of General Banks who, with his staff and bodyguard, proceeded towards the Indiana cavalry regiment, the commander of which had just sent word that the Rebel cavalry had engaged his advance.

The Confederates were to all appearances fighting for position when General Banks arrived at the front. He was told by Major Chapman of the situation, and they were discussing it when artillery firing was heard at their left and read near the Shenandoah. It was Colonel Wyndham trying to prevent the Rebel cavalry from crossing the river.

When the firing was heard by the Confederates, who were coming from the south by way of the Columbia Furnace, they at once commenced to crowd forward with vigor. The Federals were attacked in front and on the left by a superior force.

Orders were given to Chapman to fall back towards New Market, opposing as strong a resistance as possible. General Banks with his staff and bodyguard rode rapidly towards the left, where Colonel Wyndham was engaged, and on arriving there found the struggle growing. The regiment of Ashby's Black Horse was crossing the river in detachments at various points; already several had crossed successfully, and at once opened the fight.

The Confederates had some artillery with them and opened on Wyndham's battery, which they soon silenced. The numbers were in favor of Jackson, and the attack was well planned. No infantry was to be seen; it was a regular cavalry fight and Banks was in the thickest of it.

At times surrounded, but every time cutting the way through, our friends were doing all that the bravest could possibly do, but without avail. They kept close to the general, and saved him several cuts. Both Athos and Aramis were slightly wounded with saber while shielding Banks.

Our friends left the field with the general at about two o'clock, orders having been given to Colonel Wyndham to concentrate his forces. He fought a hard fight, falling back in good order. It was a retreat as yet, the rout commenced late the next day.

General Banks did not know what fear was. Neither did he know what fighting a battle was; it was not his profession. Major generals are not made in one day. He lacked initiative; would follow the advice of this man, of that man, without consulting or asserting his own judgement. It cannot be said that he became confused; he simply did not know what to do, with the exception of remaining on the field as long as the next one, unmindful of shot or shell. He would not even draw his sword, nor take pistol in hand, ready to die right there if necessary.

In the Red River campaign [of 1864,] near Sabine Cross Roads, he was exposed to the most terrible fire, staying with his men as long as his men would stay, and falling back with them in the most placid manner, as if nothing at all was the matter. That he was not killed several times, if this were possible, is a wonder. . . .

The same day when Banks and his bodyguard reached Woodstock at about six o'clock, our friends asked his leave to proceed to Washington by way of Front Royal and the Manassas Railroad.

"We would like to remain with you, General," said Athos, "but I do not see that we can help you."

"I think you better go," said the general, "however much I would like to keep such fighters as you with me, for unless I am reinforced, I cannot stop short of the Potomac, and in case you should be taken it would go hard with you."

"We are determined not to be taken again, General, as you may be convinced, after having seen us at work today."

"See General Shields at Front Royal; tell him what you have seen today, if he is still there. If he were only allowed to fall upon the rear of Jackson instead of going to Fredericksburg, things might turn out better."

They secured from the general an order on the quartermaster at Front Royal to give them immediate transportation to Washington.

It was miraculous how poor Lion got out of the scrape alive that day. Rolled over time and again by the horses during the fight, the poor beast was sore all over, but in the main unharmed.

After taking leave of General Banks they at once, but at their leisure, moved direct to Front Royal, stopping occasionally to rest their horses as well as themselves. It was a hard night's ride, and all that Lion could do to stand on his feet when they reached the place, as the bottoms of his paws were nearly worn out by the hard pike.

Front Royal was reached in the early morning, and Athos and Aramis had their wounds attended to; they were of no consequence. Captain Kelly of General Shields's staff was an acquaintance of all three, and they became his guests. They reported to the general with the compliments of General Banks, and told him what took place the day before.

"Gentlemen," said he, "I will prepare some dispatches for Washington, which you will do me the favor to deliver. The train will probably leave at noon, and you may reach the capital before night."

The general still had his arm in a sling in consequence of a severe wound received several weeks before when he drove General Jackson away to Harrisonburg. Returning with Captain Kelly to his quarters, they had him make arrangements with the quartermaster for the purchase of their horses.

"We will not need them now," said Aramis. "If we get commissions we can easily replace them in Washington."

"I do not know if he will buy them, as we are under marching orders, only one regiment to remain here, but I will see him right away."

They were allowed the regulation price for the horses, and received an order payable by the quartermaster in Washington.

"There!" exclaimed Aramis. "We once again belong to the infantry. But this time we will have a boxcar to ride in, and by evening we shall be once more at the National Hotel, where we shall find our trunks, and I assure you that I will be most happy to put myself in some other clothes. We look rather hard in these duds.". . .

At one o'clock our three friends found their way to the caboose of a commissary train, which at once commenced its weary pull towards Washington. They were alone in the caboose and had Lion near them, stretched out on the floor, completely fagged out, occasionally licking his sore paws.

"Never mind, old boy," said Aramis to the dog, "in a day or two you will be all right, and hereafter you are going to be the happiest of all dogs, as you surely are the best."

Our friends were as gay as possible, as can well be imagined. They were in hopes of reaching Washington in time that evening to permit them to deliver the dispatches and call on Minister Mercier.

Washington was not then much of a place, much of a mud hole, instead of a magnificent city as it is now. No Washington monument then, not even the ground upon which it now stands; it was then a boggy swamp. The dome of the capitol was not even completed. But be all this as it may, it certainly was the gayest city in America just then, and our friends returned to it content and happy, just as they had left it some six weeks before. They arrived late, too late, as might have been expected from a commissary train, to call upon any one, but they managed to secure their old rooms at the National Hotel. . . .

EPILOGUE
FROM THE YEAR 1901

THERE IS BUT LITTLE MORE TO SAY. THROUGH THE SECRETARY OF THE French legation at Washington and the French consul general at Richmond, Miss Alice Denson was, during the first week of June, advised of the safe arrival of Aramis and his friends at Washington. A letter from France recalled Aramis to the bedside of his mother in Paris.

A short time after, Athos was appointed on the staff of General Hancock, and D'Artagnan was sent west. Porthos joined the 5th U.S. Cavalry as assistant surgeon. Athos [Alfred Cipriani] was killed at Gettysburg, July 2, 1863.

In June 1865 Aramis [Maurice de Beaumont] returned to Richmond, was then married to Miss Alice at the French legation in Washington, and at once they went to Paris. He had kept his promise to her as soon as he could. Belonging to Napoléon III's military household, he was killed at the battle of Sedan in 1871.

Porthos [Armond Duclos] and D'Artagnan [Victor Vifquain] still live, hale and vigorous, notwithstanding their three score and more years. They have met several times in New York, where Porthos, who resigned from the military in 1866, practices medicine, and on such occasions they never fail to speak of their old friends, now dead and gone these many years ago.

NOTES

VICTOR VIFQUAIN: A BRIEF BIOGRAPHY

1. Portions of this brief biography of Victor Vifquain appeared in different form in Jeffrey H. Smith, *A Frenchman Fights for the Union: Victor Vifquain and the 97th Illinois* (Varna, Ill.: Patrick Publishing, 1992).

2. Register of Births of the Commune of Saint-Josseten Noode, 1836, Act 93, A.G.R.

3. A. Lederer, "Jean-Baptiste Vifquain, Great Patriot and Engineer," *Revue Amis Université Louvain* (Brussels), fasc. 3–4, pp. 51–67.

4. Ibid., p. 64–67.

5. Francis Balace, "Belgian Officers of the American Federal Army, 1861–1865," *Revue Belge Histoire Militaire* (Brussels) fasc. 4 (1969), p. 259.

6. Caroline Vifquain, "Early Days," *Nebraska Territorial Pioneers' Association: Reminiscences and Proceedings* 2 (1923), pp. 24–25.

7. J. Sterling Morton, *Illustrated History of Nebraska* vol. 1 (Lincoln, Nebr.: Jacob-North & Co., 1890), p. 431.

8. Letter from Victor Vifquain, published in the *Écho du Parlement* (Brussels), August 16, 1863.

9. Henry Cocheu, "The Demise of the D'Epineuil Zouaves," *Civil War Times Illustrated* (October 1997), p. 20; Compiled Military Service Records of Union Soldiers Who Served in Organizations from the State of New York (National Archives, Washington, D.C.).

10. Vifquain in *Écho du Parlement*.

11. Cocheu, "The Demise," pp. 20–22; Compiled Records, New York.

12. Ibid., pp. 24, 76–78.

13. Details on Cipriani's court-martial are found in Compiled Records, New York.

14. Frederick Phisterer, *New York in the War of the Rebellion, 1861–1865* (Albany: Weed, Parsons & Co., 1890), p. 414.

15. State of Illinois, *Report of the Adjutant General of the State of Illinois* vol. 5 (Springfield: Phillips Bros., State Printers, 1901), p. 488.

16. John S. Painter, ed., "Bullets, Hardtack, and Mud: A Soldier's View of the Vicksburg Campaign," *Journal of the West* 4 (April 1965), p. 130.

17. *Report of the Adjutant General*, p. 488.

18. U.S. War Department, *War of the Rebellion: A Compilation of the Official Records of the Union and Confederate Armies* (cited hereafter as *OR*), ser.1, vol. 17, part 1, p. 743.

19. *Report of the Adjutant General*, p. 466.
20. Joseph G. Bilby Jr., ed., "Memoirs of Military Service, Company G, 97th Illinois Infantry," *Military Images Magazine* (September–October 1981): 27–28.
21. Vifquain letter of February 24, 1863, to President Lincoln, in Compiled Military Service Records of Union Soldiers Who Served in Organizations from the State of Illinois (National Archives, Washington, D.C.).
22. Painter, "Bullets, Hardtack, and Mud," p. 148.
23. *Report of the Adjutant General*, 489.
24. Edwin C. Bearss, *The Vicksburg Campaign*, vol. 2 (Dayton, Ohio: Morningside Books, 1986), pp. 373–84, 579–642; and vol. 3, 753–862.
25. Compiled Records, Illinois.
26. Vifquain letter of July 5, 1863, to Colonel L. D. Martin, in Compiled Records, Illinois.
27. Vifquain letter of July 30, 1863, to Colonel L. D. Martin, including the note written by Tipton physician George Washington and the certification "on honor" by Vifquain, in Compiled Records, Illinois.
28. *OR*, ser. 1, vol. 26, part 1, p. 361.
29. Vifquain letter of September 15, 1863, to General Canby, in Compiled Records, Illinois.
30. Sources for this account of the battle at Fort Blakely include Arthur W. Bergeron Jr., *Confederate Mobile* (Jackson: Univ. Press of Mississippi, 1991), pp. 160–76, 185–87, and Phillip Thomas Tucker, "The First Missouri Confederate Brigade's Last Stand at Fort Blakeley on Mobile Bay," *Alabama Review* 42, no. 4 (October 1989), pp. 270–91.
31. *OR*, ser. I, vol. 49, part 1, pp. 201, 212, 214.
32. Ibid., p. 214.
33. C. C. Andrews, *History of the Campaign of Mobile* (New York: D. Van Nostrand, 1867), p. 24.
34. *OR*, ser. 1, vol. 49, part 1, p. 206. The fort owes its name to Josiah Blakeley, who founded a nearby town. However, the most widely accepted spelling for the fort is the shortened form, Blakely.
35. Roger D. Hunt and Jack R. Brown, *Brevet Brigadier Generals in Blue* (Gaithersburg, Md.: Olde Soldier Books, 1990), p. 635.
36. *Report of the Adjutant General*, p. 491.
37. Ibid., pp. 491–92.
38. Ibid., p. 492.
39. Victor Vifquain, "Address to the 97th Illinois Volunteers," Nebraska State Historical Society, Lincoln, Nebraska.
40. William D'Arcy, "The Fenian Movement in the United States" (Ph.D. diss., Catholic University of America, 1947), pp. 249–50.
41. Victor Vifquain, "An Appeal to Nebraska," Nebraska State Historical Society.
42. Thomas D. Thiessen, "The Fighting First Nebraska: Nebraska's Imperial Adventure in the Philippines," *Nebraska History* (Fall 1989): 213.
43. Vifquain Papers, Nebraska State Historical Society.

CHAPTER 1: IN WASHINGTON

1. Colonel Elmer E. Ellsworth, a personal friend of President Abraham Lincoln, became the first Northern martyr of the war. As part of a preemptive strike to secure strategic positions near Washington, D.C., the day after Virginia seceded from the United States, Ellsworth led his regiment in an attack on Alexandria, Virginia, on May 24, 1861. Ellsworth, who was twenty-four years old, was killed by

hotelkeeper James Jackson after tearing down a Southern flag that was flying from the roof of the Marshall House. Corporal Francis E. Brownell promptly killed Jackson. See Margaret Leech, *Reveille in Washington, 1860–1865* (New York: Harper & Brothers, 1941), pp. 80–81.

2. The narrator of this chapter is a character invented by Vifquain as a literary device for introducing the account of the three Frenchmen in Virginia.

3. Athos, Porthos, Aramis, and D'Artagnan were the central characters in *The Three Musketeers* by French novelist Alexandre Dumas, first published in 1844.

4. Union Brigadier General James Samuel Wadsworth (1807–64). See Mark M. Boatner, *The Civil War Dictionary* (New York: David McKay, 1959), p. 882.

5. Union Brigadier General James Shields (1806–79). See Boatner, *Civil War Dictionary*, p. 752.

6. Union Major General Nathaniel Prentiss Banks (1816–94). Confederate Major General Thomas Jonathan "Stonewall" Jackson (1824–63), later a lieutenant general. See Boatner, *Civil War Dictionary*, p. 432.

7. The popular National Hotel on Pennsylvania Avenue in Washington, D.C., hosted many of the leading personalities, both military and civilian, of the Civil War, including General Ulysses S. Grant. See Leech, *Reveille in Washington*, passim.

8. As a colonel in 1846, Ward Burnett was a Mexican War hero. Robert Selph Henry, *The Story of the Mexican War* (New York: Da Capo Press, 1989), pp. 340–41.

9. Confederate Brigadier General Camille Polignac (1832–1913), later a major general. A French-born aristocrat and veteran of the Crimean War, Polignac wrote to General P. G. T. Beauregard in March 1861 to offer his services to the Confederacy. See Roy O. Hatton, "Camille Polignac's Service," *Civil War Times Illustrated* (August 1980), pp. 9–13.

CHAPTER 2: ON THE WAY TO RICHMOND

1. Union Brigadier General Ambrose Everett Burnside (1824–81), later a major general. See William Marvel, *Burnside* (Chapel Hill: Univ. of North Carolina Press, 1991), pp. 1–96.

2. Henri Mercier was French minister (ambassador) to Washington from July 1860 to the end of 1863. Mercier was sympathetic to the South, leaning toward recognition of the Confederacy and perhaps even intervention if to France's advantage, but not without the British doing the same. See Daniel B. Carroll, *Henri Mercier and the American Civil War* (Princeton: Princeton Univ. Press, 1971), pp. 54–75.

3. U.S. Senator John Parker Hale, an abolitionist, of New Hampshire.

4. Union General George Brinton McClellan (1826–85). During the spring of 1862, McClellan commanded the Army of the Potomac during its unsuccessful attempt to capture Richmond. See Stephen W. Sears, *To the Gates of Richmond: The Peninsula Campaign* (New York: Ticknor and Fields, 1992), pp. 3–39, 337–56.

5. The Gironde of 1792 consisted of deputies from this department of France on the southwest coast who advocated republican principles in contrast to the radicalism of the French Revolution.

6. Lucius Licinius (Lucullus) was a Roman general and renowned epicure of the first century B.C.E.

7. During the Civil War, African-Americans, both free and slave, gave support and shelter to Unionists, Federal soldiers, and escaped prisoners, often at considerable risk to themselves.

8. The Virginia farmer, John Walker, is listed in the 1860 United States Census for Prince William County, Virginia, as a resident of Occoquan.

CHAPTER 3: A MARTIAL CONCERT

1. Stafford Court House was the county seat of Stafford County, Virginia. The term"court house" was often used as a designation for a county seat; Orange Court House (the county seat of Orange County) and Louisa Court House (county seat of Louisa County) will be encountered later in this book.

CHAPTER 4: PRISONERS OF FITZHUGH LEE

1. Vifquain's manuscript had incorrectly identified the unit as the 9th Virginia Cavalry.
2. Confederate Colonel Fitzhugh "Fitz" Lee (1835–1905) became a major general at the age of twenty-eight. The three Frenchmen were fortunate in encountering Lee, known for being a gentleman with an agreeable personality. His fun-loving nature earned him demerits at the United States Military Academy at West Point (Class of 1856) for dancing and loud disturbances at night, even while his uncle, Robert E. Lee, was serving as the academy's superintendent. French was one of his favorite and best subjects at West Point. See Boatner, *Civil War Dictionary*, 475; Fitzhugh Lee, *General Lee* (New York: Da Capo Press, 1994), pp. i–xiii.
3. Confederate General Albert Sidney Johnston (1803–62).
4. Reveille (the bugle call to wake up) and Boots and Saddles (the bugle call for preparing to move out or to fight) were used by both Union and Confederate armies.

CHAPTER 5: AT THE COTTAGE BY THE ROADSIDE

No notes

CHAPTER 6: IN FREDERICKSBURG; NEWS FROM PITTSBURG LANDING

1. The Confederacy referred to the decisive April 6–7, 1862, engagement in Hardin County, Tennessee, as the Battle of Pittsburg Landing, after a site on the west side of the Tennessee River. The North called it the Battle of Shiloh, the name of a nearby Methodist church. The first day of the battle was a Confederate success as the forces of General Albert Sidney Johnston caught General Ulysses S. Grant and his Army of the Tennessee by surprise, though Johnston was killed and General P. G. T. Beauregard assumed command. See Wiley Sword, *Shiloh: Bloody April* (New York: William Morrow & Co., 1974), pp. 115, 270–73.
2. "Maryland, My Maryland" was one of the most popular songs in the Confederacy, especially for the Marylanders in gray who sought to wrest their state from Union control. See W. W. Goldsborough, *The Maryland Line in the Confederate Army* (Gaithersburg, Md.: Olde Soldier Books, 1987), pp. 1–9.
3. Polignac was fine, as the Frenchmen later learned. Polignac had been in Richmond at the time of the Battle of Shiloh and did not leave the Confederate capital until April 10. See "Polignac's Diary: Part 1," *Civil War Times Illustrated* (August 1980), p. 14.
4. Union Major General Irvin McDowell (1818–85). See Boatner, *Civil War Dictionary*, p. 531.

CHAPTER 7: THE FIELD OF BATTLE

1. The Confederate success on the first day of the Battle of Shiloh (Battle of Pittsburg Landing) turned to defeat on the second day in the face of a Union counterattack. Union Major General Don Carlos Buell and his Army of the Ohio arrived on the

night of April 6, 1862, joining with General Grant's forces in the next day's successful offensive. See James McDonough, *Shiloh: In Hell Before Night* (Knoxville: Univ. of Tennessee Press, 1977), pp. 196–213.

2. Union Generals William T. Sherman, Lew Wallace, and Benjamin M. Prentiss were division commanders of Grant's Army of the Tennessee. See McDonough, *Shiloh*, pp. 226–33.

3. The battle of Champion Hill, Mississippi, on May 16, 1863, was the most decisive engagement of General Grant's campaign against Vicksburg, Mississippi. Hoping to capitalize on his Champion Hill sucess against Vicksburg's guardian army under Confederate Lieutenant General John C. Pemberton, Grant gambled on a quick capture of Vicksburg by hurling his troops against that city's powerful fortifications on May 19 and 22, resulting in high casualties and no gains. (Vifquain's manuscript had incorrectly stated that the assaults also took place on May 20 and 21.) Pemberton finally surrendered Vicksburg to Grant on July 4. See Edwin C. Bearss, *The Vicksburg Campaign* vol. 2 (Dayton, Ohio: Morningside Books, 1986), pp. 559–642; and vol. 3, pp. 753–869.

4. During the Crimean War (1853–56) between Russia and an alliance of Britain, France, and Turkey, the city of Sebastopol endured a lengthy siege before it was captured by the allies.

CHAPTER 8: IN LIBBY PRISON

1. Confederate Major General Gustavus Woodson Smith (1822–96) was known as a toughcharacter, stern, impersonal, and autocratic—in many ways the opposite of the engaging Colonel Fitzhugh Lee encountered two days earlier by the three Frenchmen. See Douglas Southall Freeman, *Lee's Lieutenants* vol. 1 (New York: Charles Scribner's Sons, 1942), p. xl.

2. Confederate Brigadier General John Henry Winder (1800–65) served for forty years in the United States Army before joining the Confederacy. Among his duties as provost marshal and prison commandant at Richmond was one especially important to the three Frenchmen: He was in charge of counterespionage in Richmond, appointing detectives who focused their attention on civilian cases. At that time, many Union loyalists in Richmond were French. The Richmond area was the center for espionage in the Confederacy, teeming with both Federal spies and foreigners, who were looked upon as one and the same by many Southerners. See Boatner, *Civil War Dictionary*, pp. 940–41; Alan Axelrod, *The War Between the Spies: A History of Espionage During the American Civil War* (New York: Grove Atlantic, 1992), p. 35; Arch Fredric Blakey, *General John H. Winder, C.S.A.* (Shippensburg, Pa.: White Maine, 1990), pp. 119–201; Edwin C. Fishel, *The Secret War for the Union: The Untold Story of Military Intelligence in the Civil War* (New York: Mariner Books, 1996), pp. 55–56, 85–101.

3. Horace Greeley, editor of the *New York Tribune*, helped raise the Federal battle cry of "On to Richmond." See Stephen W. Sears, *George B. McClellan: The Young Napoleon* (New York: Ticknor and Fields, 1988), pp. 118, 126, 136, 154.

4. Libby Prison, formerly a warehouse for Libby & Son ship chandlers, was turned into a place of captivity by General Winder in March 1862. As Richmond's primary prison for Union soldiers, it earned a notoriety second only to the Confederacy's Andersonville Prison in Georgia. Libby Prison was dismantled and shipped to Chicago in 1889 to serve as a war museum. See Richard M. Lee, *General Lee's City: An Illustrated Guide to the Historic Sites of Confederate Richmond* (McLean, Va.: EPM Publications, 1987), pp. 109–11.

CHAPTER 9: ON PAROLE IN RICHMOND

1. Captain George Washington Alexander resigned from the United States Navy in 1861 to join the Confederacy. The captain of a Confederate blockade runner, he was captured in July 1861 on the Maryland shore, charged with treason and piracy, and imprisoned at Fort McHenry, but then escaped with the help of his wife. The ankle injury sustained in the escape made him unfit for combat duty, and he joined the staff of General Winder in Richmond in 1862. Later that year he became superintendent of Castle Thunder, a Richmond tobacco warehouse turned prison. See Blakey, *General John H. Winder*, pp.144–45; Ernest B. Ferguson, *Ashes of Glory: Richmond at War* (New York: Alfred Knopf, 1996), pp. 120–21.

2. Vifquain's manuscript had incorrectly stated that Alexander broke his arm.

3. Apparently unknown to the Frenchmen, knowledge of their sudden appearance at the Confederacy's capital had reached top levels of the Confederate government. Secretary of War George W. Randolph wrote to General Winder on April 16 about the three men (misspelling the names of Cipriani and Vifquain): "You will cause the three French officers, de Beaumont, Cypreini and Vifguerin, to be carried before the court of inquiry now in session under an order obtained if necessary from the Adjutant-General. The inquiry with respect to them may be the same as in the case of political prisoners." See the Randolph letter of April 16, 1862, in *OR*, ser. 2, vol. 2, pp. 1422–23. Vifquain's manuscript makes no mention of a court of inquiry, and the three men apparently never appeared before such a body.

4. Confederate forces were preparing to meet the army of General McClellan, who had laid siege to Yorktown on the Virginia Peninsula and planned to push on toward Richmond. See Sears, *To the Gates of Richmond*, pp. 40–62.

5. Major James F. Denson, formerly a member of the First Virginia State Reserves, lived in Richmond. See the 1860 Virginia Census; 1860 Richmond City Directory, p. 83; Janet Hewett, ed., *Roster of Confederate Soldiers, 1861–1865* vol. 4 (Wilmington, N.C.: Broadfoot Publishing Company, 1996), pp. 502.

CHAPTER 10: PLAN FOR THE KIDNAPPING

1. Norfolk was a day's boat travel down the James River from Richmond. The Union's Fortress Monroe occupied the southeasternmost point of the Virginia Peninsula, only several miles from Norfolk on the other side of Hampton Roads (where the James, Nansemond, and Elizabeth Rivers unite to flow into Chesapeake Bay).

2. Vifquain explains later that he hopes to assure the cooperation of the blacks on the boat with gold and the promise of freedom.

3. The French national anthem was one of the most popular songs in the Confederacy, which closely identified with the revolutionary movements of both America and France. See Emory M. Thomas, *The Confederate Nation, 1861–1865* (New York: Harper & Row Publishers, 1979), pp. 37–38.

CHAPTER 11: MR. MERCIER IN RICHMOND

1. The tobacco transaction was a cover for Mercier's real purpose in visiting Richmond. Mercier, sympathetic to the South, had requested from U.S. Secretary of State Seward an opportunity to personally gauge the mood of the people of Richmond as part of assessing the chances that the Confederacy could prevail. After his six-day visit, Mercier concluded that the North was becoming a world power, and he did not recommend that France recognize the Confederate States of America as a sovereign nation. See Daniel B. Carroll, "A Frenchman Visits Richmond," *Civil*

War Times Illustrated (July 1971): 32-39; Carroll, *Henri Mercier*, pp. 58–59, 146–48, 167, 172–73.

CHAPTER 12: THE FLOWERS
No notes

CHAPTER 13: MR. MERCIER LEAVES

1. The CSS *Virginia* was the ironclad naval vessel created by the Confederacy out of the captured remains of the USS *Merrimack*. The *Virginia* had waged its celebrated battle with the Union ironclad USS *Monitor* on March 9, 1862, in Hampton Roads and was undergoing repairs at Norfolk. See William C. Davis, *Jefferson Davis: The Man and His Hour, A Biography* (New York: Harper Perennial, 1992), p. 412; William C. Davis, *Duel Between the First Ironclads* (Baton Rouge: Lousiana State Univ. Press, 1981), pp. 1–2, 23, 29.

CHAPTER 14: THE HEART BOWED DOWN
No notes

CHAPTER 15: A VISIT TO THE TUG
No notes

CHAPTER 16: ARAMIS AND ALICE

1. General McClellan's Army of the Potomac of more than 100,000 men outnumbered General Lee's Army of Northern Virginia by at least two to one. See Grady McWhiney and Perry D. Jamieson, *Attack and Die: Civil War Tactics and the Southern Heritage* (Tuscaloosa: Univ. of Alabama Press, 1982), p. 19. Captain Alexander's inaccurate statement of relative military strength was either an honest error or disingenuous.

CHAPTER 17: CONFESSIONS OF LOVE

1. As stated in note 1 to chapter 16, the true number of Rebel troops was closer to half that number.

CHAPTER 18: JOHN WALKER

1. Confederate Major General John Bankhead "Prince John" Magruder (1810–71) retreated from Yorktown after holding General McClellan's army at bay for a month. The Confederates on the Virginia Peninsula made their next stand at Williamsburg. See Boatner, *Civil War Dictionary*, p. 501.
2. The McClellan saddle was designed before the war by the man now leading the Army of the Potomac toward Richmond, General McClellan.

CHAPTER 19: THE GREAT NAVAL BATTLE

1. The United States Naval Academy is located at Annapolis, Maryland.
2. The armored casemate was some four inches thick; the casemate walls were actually at an angle of forty degrees. See Davis, *Duel Between the First Ironclads*, pp. 10–11, 30–31.
3. Captain Buchanan was firing a rifle from the deck of the *Virginia* and he was struck in the thigh by a bullet fired by a Union sharpshooter on shore. See Davis, *Duel Between the First Ironclads*, p. 103.

4. With Captain Buchanan wounded, the *Virginia* was commanded on this day by its executive officer, Lieutenant Commander Catesby Jones. See Patricia L. Faust, ed., *Historical Times Illustrated Encyclopedia of the Civil War* (New York: HarperCollins, 1991), p. 401.

5. The *Virginia* continued in service despite periods of repair work. See Davis, *Duel Between the First Ironclads*, pp. 138–50.

6. Vifquain in his manuscript had incorrectly stated the date as May 10.

CHAPTER 20: LAST DAY IN RICHMOND

1. Confederate Major General James Longstreet (1821–1904) commanded a division of the Army of Northern Virginia and led the rear guard during the army's fighting withdrawal up the Virginia Peninsula toward Richmond. See Boatner, *Civil War Dictionary*, pp. 928–29, 490–91; Sears, *To the Gates of Richmond*, p. 65–86.

2. Richmond was besieged by panic, with General McClellan's advance toward Richmond seeming at that time to be unstoppable. Many Richmonders fled the city for the safety of the countryside. By early May, the Confederate Congress had adjourned, the War Department archives were boxed for shipment, and the Treasury Department prepared to evacuate its gold reserves. President Davis sent his family to North Carolina. See Sears, *To the Gates of Richmond*, p. 87.

3. Norfolk fell to Federal forces on May 9, 1862, but the Confederates did not destroy their ironclad, the *Virginia*, until May 11. The explosion of the ship's magazine off Craney Island, just northwest of Norfolk, was heard for miles. See Davis, *Duel Between the First Ironclads*, pp. 138–55.

4. St. Anthony, a hermit, founded a fraternity of ascetics who lived in the desert.

CHAPTER 21: AWAY FROM RICHMOND

1. The 1860 and 1870 United States Census for Henrico County, Virginia, lists a John C. Stanard in Richmond. It is not known if this was the John Stannard of Vifquain's story, but as a plantation owner, he may have maintained a residence in the city while owning an estate in the country.

2. Confederate Major General Richard Stoddert Ewell (1817–72), later a lieutenant general; Ewell commanded a division of Stonewall Jackson's army.

CHAPTER 22: FIGHT AT THE MANSION

1. Stonewall Jackson was about to launch his famous Shenandoah Valley campaign in an effort to take pressure off Richmond and the Army of Northern Virginia during its showdown with General McClellan's Federal army. Jackson's objective was to keep General Banks's forces locked up in the Shenandoah Valley and far from Richmond so they could not join in the Union push toward the Confederate capital. See Boatner, *Civil War Dictionary*, pp. 739–41.

2. Although Vifquain's manuscript places the Stannard plantation near Orange Court House, the actual location may have been closer to present-day Stanardsville. The logistics of the Frenchmen's night-time exploratory trip to the Shenandoah River and their return the next day to cross over to Federal lines makes the Stanardsville area a more likely location.

CHAPTER 23: THE DEATH OF WALKER

1. Bandits were common in the hills of wartime Virginia, and the actual identity of Red Tom is not known. This chapter most likely is wholly fictional.

CHAPTER 24: THE GAP

1. The gap used by John appears to have been Swift Run Gap, a route through Blue Ridge in northwestern Virginia, on the east side of the Shenandoah River's south fork.

CHAPTER 25: ALICE ARRIVED

1. Although Vifquain did not include the incident in his manuscript, the three Frenchmen encountered a Confederate regiment as they moved into Swift Run Gap. A Confederate officer, Randolph H. McKim, describes in a postwar memoir how "there came to our camp here three Frenchmen whose errand and whose identity much mystified us. One of them, de Beaumont, claimed to be an officer in the Chasseurs d'Afrique. They were suspected of being spies, but we had no proof." The Frenchmen were allowed to proceed through the gap. See Randolph H. McKim, *A Soldier's Recollections: Leaves from the Diary of a Young Confederate* (New York: Longmans, Green, and Co., 1910), pp. vii, 87; John H. Worsham, *One of Jackson's Foot Cavalry* (Wilmington, N.C.: Broadfoot Publishing, 1987), pp. 41–42.

CHAPTER 26: CROSSING THE SHENANDOAH

1. Union Brigadier General Philip Henry Sheridan (1831–88), later a full general. Sheridan's ride to the battlefront at Cedar Creek on October 19, 1864, turned near defeat into victory over the forces of Lieutenant General Jubal Early. One of General Grant's top commanders, Sheridan grasped the importance of total warfare in order to bring total victory, a policy he pursued against the people and the Confederate forces of the Shenandoah Valley from summer 1864 to early 1865. See Boatner, *Civil War Dictionary*, pp. 747–48; Roy Morris, Jr., *Sheridan: The Life and Wars of General Phil Sheridan* (New York: Random House, 1992), pp. 182–221.
2. Confederate Brigadier General Turner Ashby (1828-62) was Stonewall Jackson's top cavalry commander during the Shenandoah Valley campaign. He was killed June 6, 1862, during rearguard fighting near Harrisonburg, Virginia.

CHAPTER 27: UNDER THE OLD FLAG

1. George Henry Chapman (1832–82) was a major of the 3rd Indiana Cavalry, which occupied this advance Union outpost. (Vifquain incorrectly remembered Chapman as being a colonel.) Chapman was later promoted to colonel and then brigadier general. See Boatner, *Civil War Dictionary*, p. 140.
2. Colonel Wyndham was Sir Percy Wyndham, an English nobleman, in command of the First New Jersey Volunteer Cavalry. SEe Edward Longacre, "Profile: Sir Percy Wyndham," *Civil War Times Illustrated* (December 1968): 12–15.
3. Union Brigadier General Cuvier Grover (1828–85). See Boatner, *Civil War Dictionary*, p. 363.

EPILOGUE

No notes

BIBLIOGRAPHY

PRIMARY SOURCES

Compiled Military Service Records of Union Soldiers Who Served in Organizations From the State of Illinois, National Archives, Washington, D.C.
Compiled Military Service Records of Union Soldiers Who Served In OrganizationsFrom the State of New York, National Archives, Washington, D.C.
Compiled Military Service Records of Confederate Soldiers Who Served In Organizations From the State of Missouri, National Archives, Washington, D.C.
Register of Births of the Commune of Saint-Josseten Noode, 1836, Act 93., A.G.R.
Victor Vifquain Papers. Nebraska State Historical Society, Lincoln, Nebraska.

PRIVATE COLLECTIONS
Vifquain Family Papers. Jeffrey H. Smith, Omaha, Nebraska.

NEWSPAPERS
Sunday World-Herald Magazine, Omaha, Nebraska, 4 March 1962.

BOOKS AND ARTICLES

Andrews, C. C. *History of the Campaign of Mobile*. New York: D. Van Nostrand, 1867.
Axelrod, Alan. *The War Between the Spies: A History of Espionage During the American Civil War*. New York: Grove Atlantic, 1992.
Balace, Francis. "Belgian Officers of the American Federal Army, 1861-1865." *Revue Belge Histoire Militaire* (Brussels), fasc. 4 (1969).
Ballard, Michael B. *Pemberton, A Biography*. Jackson: University Press of Mississippi, 1991.
Bearss, Edwin C. *The Vicksburg Campaign*. 3 vols. Dayton, Ohio: Morningside Books, 1986.

Bergeron, Arthur W., Jr. *Confederate Mobile*. Jackson: University Press of Mississippi, 1991.

Bilby, G. Joseph, Jr. "Memoirs of Military Service, Company G, 97th Illinois Infantry," *Military Images Magazine* (September-October 1981).

Blakey, Arch Fredric. *General John H. Winder, C.S.A.* Shippensburg, Pa.: White Mane, 1990.

Boatner, Mark M. *The Civil War Dictionary*. New York: David McKay, 1959.

Carroll, Daniel B. "A Frenchman Visits Richmond." *Civil War Times, Illustrated* (July 1971).

_____. *Henri Mercier and the American Civil War*. Princeton: Princeton University Press, 1971.

Clifford, Hopewell. *James Bowie, Texas Fighting Man*. Austin: Eakin Press, 1994.

Cocheu, "The Demise of the D'Epineuil Zouaves," *Civil War Times Illustrated* (October 1997).

Conrad, James Lee. *The Young Lions: Confederate Cadets at War*. Mechanicsburg, Pa.: Stackpole Books,1997.

D'Arcy, William. "The Fenian Movement in the United States." Ph.D. Diss., Catholic University of America, 1947.

Davis, William C. *Battle of Bull Run*. Baton Rouge: Lousiana State University Press, 1977.

_____. *Jefferson Davis: The Man and His Hour, A Biography*. New York: Harper Perennial, 1992.

_____. *The Battle of New Market*. Garden City, N.J.: Doubleday, 1975.

_____. *The Images of War, 1861-1865*. 6 vols. New York: Doubleday, 1982.

Dumas, Alexandre. *The Three Musketeers*. trans. Lowell Bair. New York: Bantam Books, 1984.

Faust, Patricia L., ed. *Historical Times Illustrated Encyclopedia of the Civil War*. New York: HarperCollins, 1991.

Ferguson, Ernest B. *Ashes of Glory: Richmond at War*. New York: Alfred Knopf, 1996.

Fishel, Edwin C. *The Secret War For The Union: The Untold Story of Military Intelligence in the Civil War*. New York: Houghton Mifflin, Mariner Books, 1996.

Foster, Gaines M. *Ghosts of the Confederacy: Defeat, the Lost Cause, and the Emergence of the New South*. Oxford: Oxford University Press, 1987.

Freeman, Douglas Southall. *Lee's Lieutenants*. 3 vols. New York: Charles Scribner's Sons, 1942.

Gaddy, David W. "Gray Cloaks And Daggers." *Civil War Times Illustrated* (July 1975).

Gallagher, Gary W., ed., *Fighting for the Confederacy: The Personal Recollections of General Edward Porter Alexander*. Chapel Hill: University of North Carolina Press, 1989.

Goldsborough, W. W. *The Maryland in the Confederate Army*. Gaithersburg, Md.: Olde Soldier Books, 1987.

Goolrick, John T. *The Story of Stafford, A Narrative History of Stafford County, Virginia*. Fredericksburg,Va.: Fredericksburg Press, 1988.

Hatton, Roy O. "Camille Polignac's Service, The Prince And The Confederates." *Civil War Times Illustrated* (August 1980).

Henry, Robert Selph. *The Story of the Mexican War*. New York: Da Capo Press, 1989.

Hewett, Janet, ed. *Roster of Confederate Soldiers, 1861-1865*. 4 vols. Wilmington, N.C.: Broadfoot Publishing Company, 1996.

Hunt, Roger D. and Jack R. Brown. *Brevet Brigadier Generals in Blue*. Gaithersburg, Md.: Olde Soldier Books, 1990.

Hurst, Harold W. *Alexandria on the Potomac, The Portrait of an Antebellum Community*. Lanham, Md.: University Press of America, 1991.

Kerby, Robert L. *Kirby Smith's Confederacy, The Trans-Mississippi South, 1863-1865.* Tuscaloosa: University of Alabama Press, 1972.

Lederer, A. "Jean-Baptiste Vifquain, Great Patriot and Engineer." *Revue Amis University Louvain* (Brussels) fasc. 3-4 (1983).

Lee, Fitzhugh. *General Lee.* ed. Gary Gallagher. New York: Da Capo Press, 1994.

Lee, Richmard M. *General Lee's City: An Illustrated Guide to the Historic Sites of Confederate Richmond.* McLean,Va.: EPM Publications, 1987.

Leech, Margaret. *Reveille in Washington, 1860-1865.* New York: Harper & Brothers Publishers, 1941.

Longacre, Edward. "Profile: Sir Percy Wyndham." *Civil War Times Illustrated* (December 1968).

Ludwell, H. Johnson. *Red River Campaign: Politics and Cotton in the Civil War.* Kent, Ohio: Kent State University Press, 1993.

McDonough, James. *Shiloh: In Hell Before Night.* Knoxville: University of Tennessee Press, 1977.

McDowell, John E. "Nathaniel P. Banks; Fighting Politico." *Civil War Times Illustrated* (January 1973).

McKim, Randolph H. *A Soldier's Recollections: Leaves from the Diary of a Young Confederate.* New York: Longmans, Green, and Co., 1910.

McLaughlin, Jack. *Jefferson and Monticello, The Biography of a Builder.* New York: Henry Holt, 1988.

McWhiney, Grady and Perry D. Jamieson. *Attack and Die: Civil War Tactics and the Southern Heritage.* Tuscalosa: University of Alabama Press, 1982.

Marvel, William. *Burnside.* Chapel Hill: University of North Carolina Press, 1991.

Meyer, Duane G. *The Heritage of Missouri.* St. Louis: River City Publishers, 1988.

Morris, Roy, Jr. *Sheridan: The Life and Wars of General Phil Sheridan.* New York: Random House, 1992.

Morton, J. Sterling. *Illustrated History of Nebraska.* 3 vols. Lincoln, Nebr.:, Jacob North & Co., 1890.

Painter, John S., ed. "Bullets, Hardtack, and Mud: A Soldier's View of the Vicksburg Campaign." *Journal of the West* 4 (April 1965).

Parks, Joseph H. *General Edmund Kirby Smith, C.S.A.* Baton Rouge: Louisiana State University Press, 1982.

Phisterer, Frederick. *New York in the War of the Rebellion, 1861-1865.* 5 vols. Albany, N.Y.: Weed, Parsons & Co., 1890.

"Polignac's Diary—Part I," *Civil War Times Illustrated* (August 1980).

"Polignac's Diary—Part II," *Civil War Times Illustrated* (October 1980).

Robertson, James I., Jr. *The Stonewall Brigade.* Baton Rouge: Louisiana State University Press, 1963.

Ryan, David D. *A Yankee Spy in Richmond: The Civil War Diary of "Crazy Bet" Van Lew.* Mechanisburg, Pa.: Stackpole Books, 1996.

Sears, Stephen W. *Chancellorsville.* Boston: Houghton Mifflin, 1996.

_____. *George B. McClellan: The Young Napoléon.* New York: Ticknor and Fields, 1988.

_____. *To The Gates of Richmond: The Peninsula Campaign.* New York: Ticknor and Fields, 1992.

Smith, Jeffrey H. *A Frenchman Fights for the Union: Victor Vifquain and the 97th Illinois.* Varna, Ill.: Patrick Publishing, 1992.

State of Illinois. *Report of the Adjutant General of the State of Illinois.* Springfield: Phillips Bros., State Printers, 1901.

Sword, Wiley. *Shiloh: Bloody April.* New York: William Morrow & Co., 1974.

Symonds, Craig L. *Joseph E. Johnston: A Civil War Biography*. New York: W. W. Norton & Co., 1992.

Thiessen, Thomas D. "The Fighting First Nebraska: Nebraska's Imperial Adventure in the Philippines." *Nebraska History* (Fall 1989).

Thomas, Emory M. *The Confederate Nation, 1861-1865*. New York: Harper & Row Publishers, 1979.

Tucker, Phillip Thomas. "The Missouri Brigade's Last Stand at Fort Blakeley on Mobile Bay." *Alabama Review* 42 no. 4 (October 1989).

Turner, George Edgar. *Victory Rode The Rails: The Strategic Place of the Railroads in the Civil War*. Lincoln: University of Nebraska Press, 1992.

Tyler, Ronnie C. *Santiago Vidaurri and the Southern Confederacy*. Austin: Texas State Historical Association, 1973.

U. S. War Department. *War of the Rebellion: A Compilation of the Official Records of the Union and Confederate Armies*. 128 vols. Washington, D.C.: Government Printing Office, 1880-1901.

Vifquain, Caroline. "Early Days." *Nebraska Territorial Pioneers' Association: Reminiscences and Proceedings* 2 (1923).

Vifquain, Victor. Letter. *Écho du Parlement* (Brussels) (16 August 1863).

Williams, T. Harry. *P. G. T. Beauregard: Napoleon in Gray*. Baton Rouge:, Louisiana State University Press, 1955.

Woodward, C. Vann, ed. *Mary Chesnut's Civil War*. New Haven, Conn.: Yale University Press, 1981.

Worsham, John H. *One of Jackson's Foot Cavalry*. Wilmington, N.C.: Broadfoot Publishing Company, 1987.

INDEX